HOW TO BORROW MONEY BELOW PRIME

Nelson E. Brestoff

Simon and Schuster   NEW YORK

This publication is designed to provide accurate and authoritative information in regard to the subject matter covered. It is sold with the understanding that the publisher is not engaged in rendering legal, accounting, or other professional service. If legal advice or other expert assistance is required, the services of a competent professional person should be sought.

–from a "Declaration of Principles jointly adopted by a Committee of the American Bar Association and a Committee of Publishers."

Copyright © 1985 by Nelson E. Brestoff,
A Professional Law Corporation

Published by Simon and Schuster
A Division of Simon & Schuster, Inc.

Simon & Schuster Building
Rockefeller Center
1230 Avenue of the Americas
New York, New York 10020

SIMON AND SCHUSTER and colophon are
registered trademarks of Simon & Schuster, Inc.

Designed by Levavi & Levavi
Manufactured in the United States of America
10 9 8 7 6 5 4 3 2 1

Library of Congress Cataloging in Publication Data

Brestoff, Nelson E.
    How to borrow money below prime.

    Bibliography: p.
    Includes index.
    1. Loans, Personal.   2. Prime rate.   I. Title.
HG3755.B74   1984   332.7′43   84-23534
ISBN 0-671-49439-2

To my wife, Lois, and to
my son, Daniel, with love.

Contents

Acknowledgments
and Declaration

Before I went to law school at the University of Southern California, my education consisted of an odd mix of English courses, science and engineering courses, journalism and politics. And although I greatly profited from all of these courses, I owe a particular debt to the rigors of my science and engineering education, first at UCLA and then at the California Institute of Technology. Although I never practiced as an engineer, I owe my thanks to the mathematics, physics, chemistry, and engineering professors who put up with me. I sincerely recommend science as a general education: as a foundation for nearly anything, including law and business, it is continually useful.

In my business career, I've been fortunate to know and work with people of high standing in their professions. Harold L. Katz, C.P.A. and senior partner of Katz, Fram, Kimmel & Co. (C.P.A.'s in Los Angeles), deserves a special note of thanks because Chapter 22 ("The Financial Condition of the United States") is largely a rewrite of a presentation developed by his firm. The material has been

9

incorporated in this book with their permission and my gratitude.

There are several others who, through love, friendship, and loyalty, have been sources of encouragement: my mother Dee "Parker" Brestoff Cherney and stepfather Guy Cherney, of San Francisco; and my brother Richard and my brother-in-law John Montague, both of whom provided helpful suggestions after reading the first draft; my client and friend Donald V. Moreno; Connie Collins, manager of Southwest Escrow Corporation; and Los Angeles City Controller James Kenneth Hahn.

I also write in memory of my father, Phillip F. Brestoff, who always believed in me.

No one, of course, has been a greater source of support than my wife, Lois. She's been a loving wife and mother to our son Daniel as well as my friend and business partner.

Because I can't reveal the precise details of the business dealings of my clients and myself without breaching the attorney-client privilege or the trust of the banking executives with whom I've worked, I can only do the next best thing:

DECLARATION

"I declare under penalty of perjury as follows:

In 1982, I borrowed $37,500 at 5 percent *below* the then-prevailing prime rate and my negotiations resulted in a loan to a client for $85,000 at 5 percent *below* the then-prevailing prime rate (16½ percent).

In 1983, I borrowed $6,000 (an equipment loan), $8,000 (a car loan), $45,000 (a second mortgage on our home), and $125,000 (unsecured) at 4 percent *below* the then-prevailing prime rate (11½ percent).

In 1984, I borrowed or negotiated loans of more than $800,000 at 4 percent *below* the then-prevailing prime rate (11¾ percent).

All of these loans were from onshore California banks. There were no points paid and no pledges or collateral other than the cars, equipment and real estate involved."

s/ _____
NELSON E. BRESTOFF
Attorney at Law

Member FDIC

$ __37,500.00_____   Loan No. __UT_____

_____Los Angeles_____, California, __December 31___, 19_81_.

On demand, or if no demand, on ____February 4, 1982____ for value received,

the undersigned jointly and severally promise to pay to ____, or order, at its ____West Los Angeles_____

____Regional Head_____ Office in the City of ____Los Angeles_____, California

*   *   *   *THIRTY-SEVEN THOUSAND FIVE HUNDRED AND NO/100*   *   *_DOLLARS,

with interest on unpaid principal from ____January 5, 1982____ at the rate of * * *FIVE* * * *____percent

__5.00___ %) per annum ~~above~~ below the prime rate of interest which the Bank charges corporate borrowers of the highest credit standing for short-term unsecured loans, which rate may change from time to time. Any changes in said prime rate shall become applicable to this note on the effective date of the change in said prime rate. Interest is computed hereunder on the basis of a 360-day year and actual days elapsed. Interest is

payable ____at maturity____, beginning ____February 4____, 19_82_. There is a minimum interest charge of $ __50.00___.

After demand, or if no demand, then after maturity, any principal remaining outstanding shall bear interest at a rate of interest which is five percent (5%) per annum higher than the interest rate specified above, which interest shall also be computed on the basis of a 360-day year and actual days elapsed. Principal and interest payable in lawful money of the United States.

The makers, sureties, endorsers, and guarantors hereof, agree: (1) to pay all cost of collection, including reasonable attorney's fees, incurred in the collection of this note; (2) to renewals and extensions of time at or after the maturity hereof; (3) to waive diligence, presentment, protest, notice of protest, demand, and notice of dishonor; (4) to waive the right to plead any statute of limitations as a defense to any claim hereunder or in connection with any security herefor to the full extent permitted by law; (5) that no failure on the part of the holder of this note to exercise any power, right or privilege hereunder, or to insist upon prompt compliance with the terms hereof, shall constitute a waiver thereof.

Nelson E. Brestoff
Lois M. Brestoff

L 541 (Rev 4/80) PS Commercial Straight Note (Interest Tied to Prime)

Foreword

"The more you know about borrowing money,
the less it will cost you."

In the last several years, interest rates have been on a roller coaster. And like the newer theme parks and their monster rides, the climbs were steep and the drops were fast. The difference, of course, is that the drops did not immediately follow the climbs. When rates go up, they tend to stay up. When they come down, they come down a long way, but reluctantly. During 1980, the prime rate skyrocketed to over 20 percent. By 1983, prime had dropped to 11 percent. To many people, 11 percent was a great relief. To those who recalled many years when the rates were between 6 percent and 8 percent, even 11 percent seemed bone-crunchingly high.

Unfortunately, there is absolutely nothing about our economic structure which will prevent a return to rates of 20 percent or higher still. It can happen again, just as it did in 1980 when the prime went from 15½ percent in early February to 20½ percent by mid-April, then eased to 11½ percent for most of August, only to return to 21½ percent by the end of the year.

These conditions are difficult to deal with and hard to plan for. People don't particularly like to borrow money and they are not accustomed to studying the vagaries of the money market. Yet, out of our desire for convenience and our instinctive following of the economic gurus who extoll the virtues of "leverage," we have become a society heavily dependent on credit. And although Shakespeare once said, "Neither a borrower nor a lender be: for loan oft loses both itself and friend," we borrow a lot.

Currently, most people and businesses borrow at rates above prime. Anyone borrowing at less than 1 over prime can usually be caught crowing about it at cocktail parties. Most bankers consider the prime rate to be a floor, and they hold it sacrosanct. On a standard deal, they will say that prime is a barrier not to be broken. You hear about "¾ over prime," or "½ over prime," but never "at prime" or below.

The proof of the pudding is that I have been able to repeatedly negotiate business loans from banks at rates *below* prime. I've negotiated loans at below prime rates with five different banks, some small ($60 million in assets) and some large (over $7 billion in assets).

We live in a time when high interest rates have touched so many people that everyone seems to follow the ups and downs as if the story were a soap opera. When times are tough, the need to borrow can sometimes be urgent. Borrowing at high rates simply puts you further behind the eight ball. Borrowing at 12 percent when others are paying 18 percent could be the difference between survival and bankruptcy. That's why I'm writing this book. If you make use of the concepts and techniques I'll be explaining, you might save the cost of my book by a thousandfold or more, depending on how much money is involved.

I'm not suggesting that I'm the first person who ever borrowed money below prime. But I did learn how to borrow at favorable rates in the "school of hard knocks," that venerable institution, and I can show you how to do it, too. My goal is to explain the thinking behind the profitability of your total relationship—deposits and loans—with your bank. You'll understand, after reading this book, how to get value out of assets you've previously ignored and didn't think were worth anything. And you'll be able to use these values to reduce your cost of borrowing, as I did, to rates below prime.

CHAPTER 1

Setting the Stage

Every time I give a speech or seminar to explain how I borrow money from banks at below prime rates (without a gun), I see the eyes of my audience light up. Borrowing below prime is an "impossible dream." I did it because I didn't know it was impossible. Along the way, I discovered that people have a great many beliefs about money, banking and interest rates that are erroneous and blind them to a clear understanding of what's going on. This book will explain everything I've discovered.

We are a credit-driven society. Very few transactions are all-cash deals. Almost every one of us has borrowed money one way or another for household, investment, or business reasons. Credit fuels our businesses and our social programs. Once we recognize that there are cycles for inflation, the economy, and interest rates, we adapt. We learn how to ride them. When inflation was over 10 percent a year, many of us thought we'd be smart to repay the loans we got then with those future dollars that'd be worth so much less. Now, with inflation down, at least some of us think it's a good idea to borrow to invest before inflation goes back up again. And before prime returns to 20 percent, heaven forbid.

For whatever reason, we borrow. And we've created all sorts of ways to do it. Credit cards, overdraft and special check-type credit plans, unsecured "signature" loans, lines of credit, loans secured by personal property, loans secured by accounts receivable, loans secured by real estate.

For example, when you purchase merchandise from your friendly retailer, you've got two options. You may be paying with cash which you either borrowed or got from dipping into your savings. On the other hand, you can finance your purchase with an installment sales contract. This book doesn't go into such things in detail. I won't be discussing installment sales contracts, student loans, loans from the Small Business Administration, or loans against the cash value of your life insurance.

Although my focus is commercial borrowing, it's important to spend a little time on credit cards, auto loans, and home mortgages—the loans which are so familiar.

Many of us start out with a credit card. Sometimes we get it in our own right; sometimes our parents arrange it and stand behind us. A credit card is an example of short-term lending by a merchant who sells on credit in order to make buying convenient for the customers. The bank is something of a middleman. The merchant sells to you and you produce your card. The merchant creates a paper impression of your card and gets your signature as your promise to pay. You've created an IOU. The merchant can bill you later or sell the IOU to someone else. If the latter happens, the merchant gets paid by the middleman bank or finance company and they bill you. When the bill is finally paid, the IOU is canceled because it's been cashed out.

Most people begin by getting a credit card from an oil company or a major department store. A VISA or Mastercharge card works the same way as cash (i.e., "near cash") because retailers accept the cards and quickly cash out the paper. VISA or Mastercharge pays them and bills you.

If you pay within thirty days, there's usually no interest

to pay. Even though there's a time value to the money, the retailers subsidize you in order to facilitate sales. They'll only do this to a point, however. With computers capable of tracking so many numbers, it's easy for the store to know whether you've paid last month's bill (or the minimum required) when you ask them to ring up this month's purchase. If your bill is unpaid, your credit's unavailable and you'll have to pay cash. A long history of success in meeting these short-term extensions of credit means that you've managed to live within your budget, month-in and month-out. As a result, your credit limit (the maximum amount you can borrow) can be increased. This is the beginning of, and no different than, the fancy "lines of credit" you hear mentioned in cocktail party conversation.

The short-term aspect of a credit card, from the lender's point of view, is one of its best features. There's a cost to extending credit. The merchant may have to borrow to keep appropriate levels of inventory because of the cash flow gap caused by his receivables. If those receivables get too high for too long, the borrowing costs may get out of hand too. The incoming stream is moving too slowly; the outgoing stream too quickly. Because a credit card is short-term, the interest rates can be readily adjusted to meet the situation. When prime was high, credit card interest rates were quickly raised from 12 to 18 percent (1½ percent per month).

As you can see, the decisions to lend are made repeatedly and the interest rates are, with the proper notice from the lender, easily adjusted. With credit card lending, however, the critical factor is not the rate of interest. Many people pay their bills within thirty days and pay no interest at all. In those cases, it wouldn't make any difference if the rate were 30 percent. Thus, the real control here is in the decision of whether to lend or not. The credit card is designed to make buying more convenient and the terms are really there to keep the privilege from being abused. If you abuse the terms, you have to pay cash. And then that computer never forgets that abuse. It keeps track of your credit history as it's being created. You can't erase; you can only enter our own explanation.

Your credit history is often important in applying for a car loan, a common longer-term loan, usually for 36 or 48 months. Because there's more money involved for a longer time than with a credit card, there's more risk to a lender. While your friendly car dealer wants to facilitate everybody's purchase just like your grocer or pharmacist, there's a lower risk (and lower rate) for prospective buyers with a clean history, a higher risk (and rate) for those with no history or a spotty one, and the highest risk and thus no credit at all for someone with a history of trouble.

Collateral becomes even more important when buying a home. Because a home's value is relatively stable and because the purchase of a house is such a major financial commitment, mortgage loans usually have much longer terms than car loans. A car starts depreciating in value once it's driven off the lot, but a house may go up in value and it will rarely go down. Thus, if you can offer a 20 percent down payment, and you have sufficient income to meet the loan payments, a clean credit history, and a professional appraisal of the house, a savings and loan will usually say "yes" to your mortgage application. But if you offer less collateral (i.e., a 10 percent down payment), the lender will be more wary and the cost will be higher. This is because the lender figures that a borrower controlling, say, a $100,000 house with only $10,000 might be more readily inclined, in financially stressful times, to walk away from $10,000 than someone who put down $20,000. The lender accounts for the greater risk with a higher rate or a shorter due date. Even though the payments are usually stretched out over thirty years to keep them low, a nervous lender might want the loan fully repaid in, say, five or seven years. Or he might adjust the interest rate. Variable-rate mortgages reflect an increasingly strong inclination to shy away from long-term lending. The cost of money changes too quickly these days to lend "long" on a fixed-rate basis.

In addition to variable rates and an early maturity, home mortgage lenders can also charge a fee just for making a loan. These fees, called points, are immediately booked as income to the lender. Each point consists of 1 percent of the loan amount. Because home mortgage lenders often want immediate remuneration for lending, even if the loan is for only seven years, they frequently charge points.

As you can see, borrowing a lot for a long time can be expensive. There are high hurdles just to get the loan, and more to pay for the privilege. This is the kind of borrowing with which most of us are familiar.

But borrowing is borrowing. And while I'll explain what I discovered in the context of the business dealings I've had, the principles apply to any kind of borrowing. For those of you who come to this book without any substantial experience or exposure to commercial loans, I ask only that you read slowly. You'll learn a great deal about money, banking, and borrowing. For those of you who understand business borrowing, the book will sometimes seem too basic and I ask only for your patience in those parts. But elsewhere you'll find answers to questions that even high-powered financial executives and successful, sophisticated businessmen have asked me—how I accomplished what they could not, even though I had a lot less money than they.

Commercial loans, the business or investment loans that we'll be focusing on, have long been the province of commercial banks. Until 1928, when the National City Bank of New York opened its comsumer loan department, commercial banks didn't bother with consumer loans at all. Nowadays, you can finance your car, home computer, or second-story addition through a bank's consumer loan department. Any lending officer, even one who specializes in business loans, can help you. But commercial banks, the 14,500-bank backbone of the country's financial circulatory system, still don't concentrate on consumer loans. The main business of these banks is business. (Actually, because of deregulation, banks and savings and loan associations are now almost two sides of the same coin. I may specifically refer to banks in the book, but I don't mean to exclude any institutional lender.)

There are two basic ways of dealing with a bank: secured and unsecured. A secured loan involves collateral, something of value to which the bank may look when things go wrong. Collateral is the banker's security blanket. An unsecured loan, a loan *without* collateral, is more rarely granted and more highly prized. It is, however, a bit more dangerous for both you and the bank. If you have trouble paying back a secured loan (a default), a bank might come after your car, your home, or your computer—whatever is posted as collateral.

When you put only your name on the line, everything is at risk. Everything that stands behind your name; everything you own. That becomes the collateral. But this cornucopia is outweighed by the effect of the bankruptcy laws. Banks are mere general creditors when it comes to collecting an unsecured loan. In a bankruptcy, all of the secured lenders have priority over any general creditor. Because secured lenders might get something, while unsecured lenders generally get nothing, collateral is frequently required.

Because my focus in this book is on the rate of interest being charged, the *pricing* question, I will not go into great detail in explaining collateral, primarily an *underwriting* subject (see Chapters 2 and 3). For our purposes, understanding the distinction between secured and unsecured loans will suffice.

CHAPTER 2

Borrowing Against Cash

My discovery concerning pricing lies in understanding how certain banking and financial concepts interact with each other. I discovered how a banker thinks (or should think) when he or she prices a loan.

What I discovered has nothing to do with my being an attorney. At the time I made my discovery, I was negotiating a business loan with my banker, and although the subject was real estate, it could just as well have been electronics, soybeans, or T-shirts.

Let's begin with a few basics. Many people are familiar with borrowing against cash. Usually the situation involves a long-term certificate of deposit (C.D.), say for one year, and an immediate cash need sometime before the C.D. matures. If you reach for the funds before maturity, there may be penalties, in addition to losing the high interest you expected. Recognizing this, and out of a desire to provide a service, bankers will often make loans equal to your needs because the C.D. is available as collateral. The bank now has a source of repayment and need only wait until the C.D.

matures, if necessary. When the C.D. matures, the bank can repay its own loan by virtue of the funds in the C.D.

The first point that this example demonstrates is that bankers decide whether you are a good risk for a loan (the "underwriting" decision) before they decide how much to charge for the use of their money (the "pricing" decision). In the case of a loan secured by a C.D., the underwriting question is easily answered. Bankers will always loan their own money when the funds necessary to repay them are sitting there on deposit and locked in. Cash is excellent collateral.

It was only recently that bankers were asked to make C.D. loans on a frequent basis. Before the strong effects of inflation and a two-income household, C.D.s were considered exotic instruments available only in $100,000 increments. They were only available to and suitable for the rich and financially sophisticated. Most people kept their money in thrift institutions or savings and loan associations, where they had to be satisfied with earning 5¼ percent or slightly more.

As you will soon see, banks and savings and loans want to attract your deposits, even if they have to pay for them. The competition sometimes results in full-scale advertising extravaganzas, with each institution trying to outdo the other with movie stars, high rates, and claims of better service. In a broad effort to attract your deposits in the late seventies and early eighties, the banks made the high-interest C.D. available in amounts under $100,000.

C.D.'s became more prevalent as they became available in smaller amounts. But the purchasers of C.D.'s in more modest increments weren't really wealthy. They didn't have "patient" money, money that could literally sit forever in the bank. The new owners of small-increment C.D.'s had varying needs for cash, and they often miscalculated those needs by several months. They committed too much money for too long a period of time.

So the loan requests became more frequent.

At first, bankers were willing to make these short-term loans for the same rate of interest being earned on the C.D. If the C.D. was bringing 14 percent, the loan secured by the C.D. was priced at 14 percent. For the borrower, the transaction was just like having the C.D. mature when the funds were needed. The penalties for early withdrawal were avoided and the banker had performed a service. (Actually, as you will see later, the banker did better than that).

As time went by, and such loans became even more prevalent, bankers charged 1 or 2 percent over the C.D. rate. It always seemed odd to me, though, that the banks could afford to charge nothing or so little. There were, after all, administrative costs to consider. The loan involved paperwork, review, and handling. Associated with these transaction costs were such items as electricity, rent, salaries, and taxes. If the loan was for three months (until the C.D. matured), the bank incurred all of these costs and seemed to take in essentially no income. For example, if the bank charged interest at 15 percent for a three-month, $10,000 loan against a $10,000 C.D. earning 14 percent, the bank earned only $25.[1] And in earlier days, when the interest income and interest expense exactly offset each other, it seemed like the bank was losing money.

Clue No. 1: Banks never lose money when they lend against cash.

---

1. Notice that you need to divide by 12 to deannualize a transaction for results over a period of months:

$$\frac{(\$10,000 \times 15\%) - (\$10,000 \times 14\%)}{12} \times 3 = \$25.$$

CHAPTER 3

The Underwriting Issue

Before I go on to discuss pricing in any detail, the subject of underwriting needs some attention.

In the C.D. example, the underwriting issue was simple because it was almost insignificant. Our banker didn't have to think long or hard about whether to make the loan since the source of repayment was cash on hand. Cash, as you know, speaks loudly.

When the source of repayment is not so immediately evident, our banker will want to know something about the borrower. Sometimes it seems as if the banker only wants to know two things: (1) that you can neatly fill out the detailed financial statement which the bank requires and (2) that you have a substantial net worth and a healthy income.

Initially this second test, your ability to repay the loan, is a frustrating *sine qua non* (which means "without which not"). When you need a loan it's because you don't have the cash available for what you have in mind. Yet when you have a strong need, bankers are reluctant (the good ones aren't—they try to find a way to make the loan). They wonder what the "source of repayment" will be if you don't have the cash. Conversely, when you're flush with cash and don't need a loan, bankers want to lend you the money. You can't get sidetracked by this paradox. It's just there.

Now, sometimes people try to show a greater net worth than they really have when they fill out their financial statement. Although bankers are well aware that people fudge the value of their homes, investments and jewelry, one should never grossly inflate the stated value of one's investments or make up assets one doesn't have. The financial statements are signed under penalty of perjury. Misstatements like intentionally omitting mention of a personal (i.e., unsecured) loan at another bank amounts to fraud on the lender and, perhaps, a federal crime.

Bankers do understand that your financial statement is inexact, and they know that we rarely forget assets and love to ignore liabilities. Smaller matters, of course, are more easily forgotten and more easily forgiven. Larger and seemingly intentional efforts to water your statement—to make it heavier than it really is—are downright dishonest.

The trouble with such conduct is that bankers have seen it many times before. Because your reputation is a very valuable commodity in the underwriting decision-making process, stretching your financial statement too far is penny wise and tons foolish.

What I'm getting at here is fairly obvious: next to who you are "by the numbers," the most important definition of who you are is whether people trust you. Your character and reputation are critical factors. If you have family connections, strong educational credentials, or if you've been actively involved in civic or business-related affairs, people will have some positive measure of you. You'll have met some of the movers and shakers who lead your community. Your involvement with them will ultimately lead you to rubbing shoulders with branch managers or vice-presidents from several different institutions. Your ability to cite them as references will attest to your continuing stake in the community. These are tips to your banker that you'll work tirelessly to repay his or her trust (and loan) because you already have so much invested in your own good name.

If you don't have some of the ingredients I've mentioned, there's no substitute and no shortcut. Join a chamber of commerce or civic group and work hard in your chosen committee. When you perform well in a situation like this, you meet other people in other businesses. When you help carry out a seminar series or business-high-school interaction program, you'll gain confidence in yourself and the trust of others. And you'll be showing evidence of possessing the third basic ingredient of a favorable underwriting decision: capacity.

Capacity is as important as capital and character because your banker is looking at your ability to succeed as a measure of your ability to repay the loan. He or she is certainly not going to bank on a prospective failure. The old cliché that nothing succeeds like success is true because people believe that the past is prologue. The only hint you can give them as to whether you'll succeed is whether you've succeeded before, even if your success is in a completely unrelated project. If you can be relied upon for regular, prompt attendance in your "public" performances, and enthusiastic, capable handling of tasks assigned or voluntarily chosen, your banker will have a tendency to believe in you. This is because the people you work with nod their head when asked about you. You get an O.K.

A banker's underwriting decision is whether to make a loan or not. To you. You are selling yourself and you need to focus on the three basic aspects I've mentioned: capital, character, and capacity.

Now that we've covered the elements, a word about the "packaging" is in order. Like it or not, we've never really left grade school. *You will be graded.* Each of the elements—capital, character, and capacity—will be ranked on a relative, qualitative scale. Your presentation is your first impression and it will be graded too. When I present my financial statement, I use my own format modeled on a bank's form. The bank's form is generally too confining and difficult to fill out neatly. I reference my own form on the bank's, attach it, and sign the bank's form. This should be acceptable and it generally will be allowed, especially if you show tact and ask in advance for approval.

If you have a word processor or home computer, you can store your financial statement and modify it easily enough. You gain some modicum of respect for having your own personal format. You'll be glad when you later find that it's quick and easy to update your statement and satisfy your banker's request for current information. I tend to use footnotes and provide a fair amount of explanatory text. This answers a lot of questions in advance and also allows me a convenient means of justifying my numbers.

By the way, bankers often ask for your tax returns for the last year or two. My suggestion is to keep at least two copies of each year's return in a separate file. Your banker will be impressed if you offer your returns *before* they're requested. You will only generate concern if you respond with delay or resistance. If your returns don't truly reflect your earning power because of careful tax planning, simply explain what you've done. Bankers are people, too. They understand that you may be shifting income into future years or making good use of tax shelters to reduce your adjusted gross income.

In addition to your financial statement, you might also include a one-page biography showing education, experience, honors, publications, and references. This "paperwork" is not crucial, but very helpful. I also think you ought to present yourself on good-looking stationery. To me, a biography on quality stationery often adds dimension and depth to a loan application. It's something for your banker to read and, perhaps, warm up to. As important as the numbers may be, the picture they present alone is cold and impersonal.

Assuming that your loan application will get good marks for presentation, how will your banker analyze the three Cs, capital, character, and capacity? In addition to scoring your financial statement, looking at your credit report, and considering the other two Cs—market conditions and your collateral—your banker is really trying to sniff out some reason for saying "no." You almost have to expect it as a first response.

Because of this, there's really no substitute for having some good measure of all three ingredients. Weaknesses in any one can quickly lead your banker's mind away from saying "yes." That's because all of us tend to think in selective extremes. Your banker may spot a weak point and, partially because of time pressure, tend to magnify the negative and merely acknowledge the positive. This is really quite understandable because bankers, as money managers, must err on the side of caution, to avoid making a bad loan. Although today's bankers are more aggressively interested in finding some way to "skin the cat," they are inherently conservative. As a result, it will often seem that their favorite word is "no." With some bankers, however, this is just how they always begin negotiations.

CHAPTER 4

Leveraging by
the Bank

Now that we've explored the underwriting issue, let's set some building blocks for seeing how a banker prices a loan. One cornerstone involves understanding the system of banking in general. Banking is the business of buying money from one group of customers (depositors) and selling money to another group of customers (borrowers). In this context, we must pay particular attention to the concepts of leverage and yield.

You are "leveraged" when, instead of owning something outright, you borrow (from a banker or the seller of that something) in order to control the asset in question. You are highly leveraged when you've managed to gain control of something with a very small investment. Your "yield" on this small investment will be large even if the total value due to appreciation increases only slightly. Let's say that you bought a $100,000 house with only 5 percent or $5,000 down. If the value appreciates only 5 percent to $105,000, you've *doubled* your money. At the same time, you have little to lose if your investment goes sour. Great for you. But you also have little incentive to protect a highly leveraged investment when the storm clouds start forming. This is what scares your banker.

Although a banker may frown on you for being highly leveraged, the banking business is built on it. Because banks work with borrowed funds which are a substantial multiple of their capital, they are leveraged on a grand scale. There have been times when the equity of American banks was only a few percent. Many bankers think that 4 percent should be the maximum leverage, a ratio of assets to equity of 25 to 1.

It's these assets which earn money for the bank. For most of us, assets are things we own, like cash and real estate. For banks, a large fraction of its assets are the loans it has made. These loans are receivables, and receivables are assets. Our deposits (assets for us) are liabilities for a bank.

In short, banks make money when they lend it. Borrow and lend. Borrow and lend. The more they lend, the more they make. Provided, of course, that the underwriting decision is correct and the loan is sound.

By offering to pay interest to depositors (the C.D., for example, or by paying interest on the new money market checking accounts, for another), banks acquire money. What they pay to attract this money is their "cost of funds." Prior to deregulation, one of the predominant sources of funds was the ninety-day C.D. rate. After deregulation, C.D. deposits have a strong rival—the money market accounts. Because banks were allowed to pay interest for these checking accounts, a great deal of money was attracted away from the money market and mutual funds operated by Wall Street brokerage houses. The money market rate is usually lower than the C.D. rate and, because there's so much money involved in these accounts now, a good estimate of a bank's cost of funds is the midpoint between the ninety-day C.D. rate and the money market rate. Other sources are such mystical things as Fed funds, repos, and Eurodollars.[1] A

---

1. The term "Fed funds" refers to a transaction between banks. The lending bank has excess reserves on hand at the Fed that are earning

bank's true cost of funds is the blended result of all of these money sources.

Let's assume that a bank considers its private cost of funds to be equal to what the bank must pay to attract funds into a money market checking account. Furthermore, let's assume that this costs the bank 12 percent and that the prime rate is 16 percent.

As you can see, I'm looking at a money market account or a C.D. now from a different viewpoint than the one with which you're familiar as a depositor. You've been thinking of them as relatively high-interest financial investments. To you, they mean interest *income*. To a bank, however, they mean interest *expense*.

Let's discuss a hypothetical example. I'm going to use relatively large numbers for two reasons: first, these were the numbers I used in an actual negotiation; second, you'll understand the concepts more easily when the numbers are larger. We start by depositing $400,000. That means they are demand deposits. The bank must deposit 12 percent of this $400,000 with a Federal Reserve Bank to satisfy the reserve requirement (see Chapter 5). This means the bank can lend

---

no interest. The term is usually very short and is sometimes known as "overnight" money because it's only lent for one day. Fed funds are a vital source of income for a bank. The lending bank is liquid, but has a shortage of borrowers. The excess money is lent to another bank, one presumably with borrowers but not enough cash, and earns interest at the Fed funds rate.

"Repos" is shorthand for "repurchase agreements." A repo is the sale of money with United States government securities as collateral and a simultaneous agreement to buy the money back for a small increase (the equivalent of interest). Again, the usual term is one business day. A special case, a "continuing contract," involves automatic renewals unless terminated by either party.

"Eurodollars" are deposits, counted in United States dollars, in banks outside of the United States, even if the bank is affiliated with a United States bank. For articles discussing each of these, and other financial instruments, see Timothy Q. Cook and Bruce J. Summers, *Instruments of the Money Market* (Federal Reserve Bank of Richmond, 5th ed. 1981).

out $352,000 and probably earn 2 over prime, or 18 percent. If it does, the bank's gross interest income is $63,360 ($352,000 multiplied by 18 percent).

Assuming that the bank has charged no points, what is the yield to the bank? Well, the bank is loaning $352,000, and earning $63,360. Against this, subtract the $48,000 we earned as interest. We've given the bank an opportunity to make $15,360 based on our relationship with it. If we divide the bank's $15,360 income by the $352,000 in loans, we see that the bank is making 4.36 cents for every dollar it lends.

This yield is a 4.36 percent return-on-asset (ROA) yield, the relevant asset being the total loans made. If the ratio of assets to equity is 25 to 1, an ROA yield of 4.36 would translate into a return-on-equity (ROE) yield of *109 percent*.

Now this gross yield figure is important, but it doesn't tell the whole story. The bank's profitability is based on *net* yield, not gross. Against this interest income, the bank must pay salaries, rent and all of the other ordinary expenses of a business. It's this bottom line that counts.

Clue No. 2: an ROA yield of only 4 percent is a very good place to start. For the bank.

CHAPTER 5

Reserves From the Bank's Perspective

Allow me to digress.

From your banker's point of view, the Fed is dictating the parameters within which both you and the bank are operating, and the most powerful parameter is the reserve requirement. (We'll get to the discount rate, which is also set by the Fed, in the next chapter).

Banking regulations require banks to keep a certain percentage of demand deposits (e.g., checking accounts) on hand to pay out—on demand. Because no one expects everyone to make a demand for funds at the same time, the Federal Reserve requires a bank to keep only a percentage of its demand deposits on hand. This is known as the "reserve requirement."

If the reserve requirements are increased, for example, you need to realize that your banker has just been blitzed by the Fed. Your banker must either borrow to meet the requirements (and incur an additional cost that reduces his willingness to deal with you) or find other sources of deposits.

Let's look at what an increase in the reserve requirement might mean to your banker. First of all, any increase freezes an additional amount of the bank's assets in reserve balances that earn no interest. More importantly, any increase is magnified by leverage so that the bank's lending ability is restricted all the more.

Let's suppose that we're dealing with a small-unit (i.e., single office) bank with $10,000,000 in demand deposits, that the reserve requirement is 25 percent (for ease of illustration), and that the discount rate is 12 percent. Of course, the reserve requirement means that our bank has to have $2,500,000 in vault cash or Fed deposits. Unfortunately, our bank is reserve *deficient* and has only $2,400,000 on deposit. If our bank borrows $100,000 from the Fed to meet the reserve requirement, the cost of doing so is $12,000.

But now let's suppose that the reserve requirement is reduced to 20 percent. If this happens, the effect is a dramatic swing in fortunes. Now, with $10,000,000 in demand deposits, we only need $2,000,000 in reserves. Our bank is no longer $100,000 short, but $400,000 over the requirement. This money can either be withdrawn and lent (or used to buy securities) or left on deposit so that the bank's lending power increases by $2,000,000 ($400,000 is 20 percent of $2,000,000).

Just as the bank's opportunity to make money dramatically increases when the reserve requirement is decreased, a swing in the other direction is just as sweeping. If the reserve requirement is increased to 30 percent, we are no longer only $100,000 short. With $10,000,000 in demand deposits, we need $3,000,000 on hand with the Fed. Now we are $600,000 short. With our cost of borrowing at 12 percent, our expenses will shoot up from $12,000 to $72,000. Instead of borrowing from the Fed, our banker might go on the warpath to bring in an additional $600,000 in deposits. He or she will be emotionally depressed and financially strapped. The advertising campaigns designed to attract depositors will become even more intense. If the drive for deposits doesn't work, or is working too slowly, the bank might have to sell securities and/or call in some loans in order to scare up the necessary cash.

Since the reserve requirement is a powerful tool, it's not used nearly as often as are changes in the discount rate. From 1951 to 1970, the Fed changed the reserve requirements only fourteen times—up, five times; down, nine times. During the same period, the discount rate was changed more than thirty times. The changes are, however, within certain limits set by Congress. For time deposits (i.e., savings accounts), the range for the reserve requirement is between 3 and 10 percent. For demand deposits (i.e., checking accounts) at smaller "country" banks, the reserve requirements can vary between 7 and 14 percent. For larger, "city" banks, the Fed can require between 10 and 22 percent of demand deposits.

For the material which follows, a precise understanding of a customer's total relationship with a bank on an ROA basis is necessary. Here are the important numbers: the reserve requirement for checking accounts, whether they earn interest or not, is 12 percent; for savings accounts, the reserve requirement is 3 percent. These are the currently prevailing reserve requirements for all but the very smallest banks.

CHAPTER 6

The Discount Rate
and Open Market Operations

Wh   hen a bank has deficient reserves, it has to do
something and, generally, there are three alternatives. First,
the bank can call in loans or sell some securities to create the
cash necessary for the reserve deposit required. Second, it
can campaign for deposits. Third, because of the reluctance
to either call in loans or sell any securities, the bank can borrow the cash (just like we would).

In the Federal Reserve system, the member banks have
a relatively cheap and convenient source of funds—the Federal Reserve Bank itself. When a bank borrows from the Fed
to meet its reserve requirement, or for any other reason, it
pays interest at what is known as the discount rate. If it borrows just to meet the reserve requirement, the money supply
created by the bank stays the same. That is, the money it has
put into the marketplace, for its securities and loan portfolios, stays the same. When a bank borrows additional reserves from the Fed, it can increase these portfolios by a
substantial factor. These increases are increases in the supply
of money. The Fed influences the willingness of banks to
borrow reserves by raising or lowering the discount rate.

The manipulation of the discount rate is (along with the reserve requirement and open market operations) one of the three primary ways the Fed influences interest rates. Of the three the discount rate is probably the least influential. This is so because the Fed's action doesn't force any particular result. The initiative for borrowing from the Fed at the discount rate lies with the banks, not the Fed. A change in the discount rate only affects banks which owe money to the Fed. For those banks who consider borrowing to increase their reserves, a shift in the discount rate simply forces them to consider whether to borrow and pay the discount rate or to find some other cheaper source of additional reserves.

In addition, the Fed often views a change in the discount rate with mixed feelings because it can't predict the market's reaction. If the discount rate is increased, the market might expect a swing toward a "tight money" condition in the future. As a hedge, borrowing might surge and cause an increase in the money supply. If the Fed were trying to "tighten" things up, this is the opposite of the result intended.

While changes in the discount rate and reserve requirements are relatively infrequent and thus noticeable when they happen, the Fed also operates through an Open Market Committee. It functions so often that its effect is rarely noticed by the general public and almost never discussd by the press.

Nevertheless, if you're going to walk in the same shoes as your banker, you'll need to understand the basics of the Open Market Committee and what it does. The Open Market Committee is, in fact, a financial mechanism which is regarded as having as much, if not more, punch as a change in the reserve requirement.

What's involved is nothing less than the Fed's participation in the capital marketplace. The Fed has money which it uses to buy and sell government securities. With these operations, the Fed can move unobtrusively and gradually, even though it deals in billions of dollars.

Now, first, what are government securities? Since you

can't own stock in the United States, the government issues debt securities such as savings bonds and Treasury bills and pays investors for the use of their money. These securities are, in fact, issued to attract money from individuals, corporations, and financial institutions to finance previous budget deficits. After buying them, these holders of government securities have the certificates instead of cash. The long-term obligations are usually called bonds. The short-term paper is the now-familiar "T-bill." There is a broad market for these negotiable securities and hundreds of billions of dollars worth are available.

When the Fed goes to market, and buys securities, it pays with a check drawn on itself. It receives the security formerly held, say, by a bank. When the bank deposits the check at the Fed, it gets credited with reserves in the same amount. With the reserves, it can loan more money. If the seller is an individual, instead of a bank, there is an additional step. The Fed issues a check, the individual deposits it in his bank (and thus increases the supply of money), and the bank turns the check in for reserves. Now the money supply is up (there's money in someone's account that wasn't there before) and the bank's lending ability has gone up.

When the Fed is buying, it's trying to add money to the game and hoping that interest rates will fall. When the Open Market Committee is buying, you can expect easier credit.

But when the Fed is selling, things tighten up. Then the Fed gets a check for the securities drawn on a bank. When it cashes the check, it drains the account of the buyer and reduces the bank's demand deposits. Of course, the Fed first collects by charging the bank's reserves and then the bank charges the account of its customer. Thus, both the money supply and the bank reserves are decreased. What the Fed giveth, it can taketh away.

These transactions go on daily in large numbers. The Fed publishes weekly data on its open market operations every Thursday afternoon. The Friday newspapers carry the news. Because the moves might be to offset the effect of any number of factors, those who watch the doings at the Fed can't completely rely on the open market activity to predict changes in interest rates. In addition to open market activity, they look to movements in the T-bill rates, and lots of other factors, to second-guess the Fed's underlying goals. As you might suspect, there is more art to this than science. The outsiders are trying to read the minds of the insiders and the insiders aren't quite sure that what they're doing will result in what they're trying to do.

One little secret I can pass on, however, is that the Fed is amazingly talkative. Not so much about what's going on right at the moment, or where we're going, but about the past, even the recent past. Most branches of the Fed (there are twelve of them listed in the Appendix B) have public information departments which are stocked with educational materials, most of which are free. I walked away with an armful of free booklets, papers, reports, and brochures. Some of it is designed to explain money and banking to kids. But most of what's available deals with Fed operations, new financial instruments, new rules and regulations, and so on. Sophisticated stuff.

You can also drown in the statistics.

What's perhaps most useful is to get yourself on the mailing list of the research department of the branch near you. The San Francisco branch, for instance, publishes a weekly newsletter. There are statistics, of course, but also articles by members of the research staff on the banking issues of the day.

CHAPTER 7

Checking vs. Savings

Besides the checking account, the other banking relationship with which most people are familiar is the savings account. Bankers tend to view the savings account as a second-class citizen because of its cost.

Older banks with a large number of branches find savings accounts valuable primarily because of their sheer numbers. When a bank has a great number of savings accounts, it has a broad source of funds which only costs it roughly the rate of interest it pays. A bank with a huge consumer base of 5¼ percent savings accounts can continue to profitably make consumer loans (i.e., loans for cars, boats, office equipment, and the like) at 12 percent even though the prime rate may have gone through the roof. The leading example is the Bank of America, with over 3,000,000 personal checking and savings accounts.

Savings accounts, although not to be dismissed, are simply not perceived by the banks to have the financial advantages that demand deposits have. In reality, however, because the reserve requirement for savings accounts is even lower than the requirement for checking accounts, a substantial savings account is valuable indeed. But try persuading a banker of this. They'll always point to the interest they're paying you. It's a perceptual barrier that's very difficult to overcome.

In contrast with this perception of savings accounts, and to show you the power of a checking account, a banker once remarked to me, in all seriousness, that a $15,000 *checking* account was worth as much if not more to him (as a banker) as a *$100,000* savings account.

Why would anyone trade a savings account for a checking account? Or for that matter, trade a C.D. or other higher-earning alternative (like a money market fund or commercial paper) for one? The answer is: in order to borrow money below prime.

In order to obtain a better borrowing rate, you have to offer something to the bank. That something is (this shouldn't be a great surprise): *money*—in the form of deposits. Your checking accounts. Your savings accounts.

Most people have never thought of this kind of combined deposit/loan relationship with a bank. Most businesses, even those with strong checking accounts, don't recognize the power they have. It is indeed out of the ordinary to base a borrowing request on the amount of deposits you control. Almost everyone thinks that a checking account is just a general account which unfortunately doesn't earn interest and out of which the bills are paid. And that a savings account is merely that.

But times are changing. People are becoming more aware and sophisticated about money. Maybe it's because the record-high levels of the prime rate during 1981 and 1982 touched so many people. In any case, whether out of necessity or self-defense, people have developed a real hunger to learn more about money and how it works.

Clue No. 3: Bankers only appear to turn up their noses at checking accounts. They really *want* checking accounts more than any other type of account.

CHAPTER 8

Tax Aspects of Interest

My first recommendation for obtaining below-prime loans is that you consider the power of your checking account. This might mean giving up interest-bearing accounts in favor of non-interest-bearing checking accounts. If you doubt my sanity, please read on. This was the conceptual "shift" that those record-high levels of the prime rate forced in my thinking. Once I realized this and had actually negotiated a below prime loan, I began to see lots of reasons for having or controlling money in a checking account. Here are some of the tax and cash flow aspects which argue in favor of this.

First, the tax aspects. Hypothetically, let's assume we have $50,000 to work with during a year's time. If the money were in a savings account earning 6 percent, we'd earn $3,000 in interest income.

But interest income is ordinary income that is taxable at the margin. By this I mean that the income earned from interest is taxed at the level of the tax bracket in which you find yourself as a result of all your other work (your gross income from salaries, your itemized deductions, etc.). If your bracket at the end of the year is the maximum 50%, then your interest income is halved. You would net only $1,500, a yield (ignoring inflation) of only 3 percent.

Why do I apply the bracket rate? Because the last dollar in is taxed at the bracket rate. The next dollar in is similarly taxed unless it moves you into a higher bracket. It doesn't matter to this last dollar what the taxes have been for any previous dollar.

Because my time is spent earning salaries and finding investments, the last dollar in is a dollar earned strictly from the time value of money. So, interest income should be viewed as the last dollar received. As such, it is income earned "at the margin," and is taxed at the highest applicable rate, the bracket rate. For individuals, the maximum rate is 50 percent; for corporations, 46 percent.

When we borrow, on the other hand, we incur interest expense. For businesses, this interest expense is a fully written-off dollar, just like the cost of raw materials, rent, salaries, taxes, and so on. For individuals, however, interest expense is only partially an offset against income. For individuals, interest expense is usually incurred in connection with a home mortgage. You'll find a category for interest expense listed on Schedule A of your tax return along with others for medical expenses, taxes, contributions, casualty or theft losses, and miscellaneous. If you're married and filing a joint return or if you're a qualifying widower with a dependent child, the first $3,400 of your Schedule A deductions don't count. If you are filing as single or head of household, the first $2,300 in deductions don't count. If you are married and filing a separate return, the first $1,700 in deductions don't count.

If you are married, filing a joint return, and your only Schedule A deduction is $3,400 in interest, the money spent for interest is worthless as a deduction. If you have deductions for medical, taxes, interest, and so on, so that they add up to $34,000, the deductions are really only worth 90 cents on every dollar because the first $3,400 don't count.

Thus, assuming no other deductions, interest is not entirely useful as a write-off because not all of it counts. I can always do without an expense and I'd always prefer to do without one which is only partially deductible. Assuming no other Schedule A deductions, an interest expense is only 90% worthwhile when there's $34,000 of it ($3,400 doesn't count) and only 50% worthwhile when there's only $6,800 of it. Of course, if taxes or other Schedule A deductions exceed $3,400, then any *additional* interest expense is 100% deductible.[1]

Since both interest income and interest expense are paid or payable on a regular monthly basis, the subject of cash flow is a natural. Managing cash flow is difficult for most people. Too often people have budgeted poorly or rationalized their budgets away too quickly when something unexpected comes up. If your personal or business cash flow is tight, it may well be because your interest expenses are being increased by escalating rates. Individuals can, I believe, obtain some badly needed relief from the pressure on their cash flow by giving up interest income (which is taxed at your highest bracket rate) and reducing interest expense (which is only partially deductible). For business, the strategy is the same even though interest expense is a dollar-for-dollar offset to income.

These days, many people and most businesses need to be vitally concerned with cash flow because it is essential to financial survival, especially during times of high interest rates combined with an economic slowdown. Many of us, individuals and businesses, have been mortgaging our future by borrowing to close the cash flow gap. When the loans are due, there is another round of borrowing. This "rollover" strategy is used in order to survive, but it is very expensive if you are paying high rates.

1. If Congress passes a tax reform package that sets a limit on interest deductions (one proposed ceiling is $5,000 for deductions not involving a home mortgage), the point of this chapter has even greater force.

If business is slow for too long a time, the high cost of borrowing puts you even further behind. At some point, the interest expense becomes overwhelming and too much of your revenues must be directed toward covering the expense. It becomes difficult to allocate funds to long-term uses such as investment, retooling, or research. The only way out of this ever-worsening situation is bankruptcy or merger with someone who is cash-rich and who may want you for a bargain price.

Or, you can try to reduce your borrowing costs. The idea is to use demand deposits (and savings accounts) to increase your negotiating power with a bank because the bank can, in turn, make money with your money. The more the bank stands to make, the more it can afford to offer you to attract you as a customer. This is sometimes referred to as "compensating balances," a phrase which I dislike because it has no definition and is, in reality, misleading. As we go further, you'll see what I mean. For the moment, and especially if you're familiar with "compensating balances," please be patient.

CHAPTER 9

The Prime Rate

Before we take up an example that shows you how to convince a bank that it can afford to make a loan at rates below prime (Chapter 10), let's analyze our target. What is the prime rate?

Historically, the prime rate has been defined as the rate which the bank charges their most creditworthy customers. In reality, the prime rate is a chameleon. There are no set criteria or determining factors for it. A smaller bank in Beverly Hills, for example, with less than $100,000,000 in assets, may have a different prime rate for its customers than does the Bank of America or Citibank for their customers. Some banks tie their prime to a large West Coast bank, such as the Bank of America; others to a large bank in New York. Still others decide for themselves.

Webster's New Collegiate dictionary still defines the prime rate as

An interest rate at which preferred customers can borrow from banks and which is the *lowest commercial interest rate available at a particular time.* (Emphasis added.)

As you'll see, however, this is no longer an accurate definition.

The phrase "prime rate" took on real meaning in 1933 when a 1½ percent rate was adopted as the lowest rate for preferred customers. The prime stayed at 1½ percent for seventeen years, and was relatively stable after World War II until the seventies. See the graph in Appendix A.

When the prime began to soar in 1979–1981, Congress recognized that the high rates were causing a great deal of financial pain. Congressman Fernand J. St. Germain sent a letter to the ten largest commercial banks in the country, asking them to describe their practices and just what the banks meant by "prime." The banks might not have answered a letter from you or me, but Congressman St. Germain is chairman of the House Committee on Banking, Finance and Urban Affairs. Congressman St. Germain would certainly be sympathetic to the point I want to make in this chapter. When he transmitted the staff report[1] to the members of the committee, he had a few sharp words for the banks:

Transmitted herewith is a staff analysis of prime rate lending practices at the nation's ten largest commercial banks. . . .

This survey clearly establishes that the phrase "prime rate," which at one time stood for the absolute lowest available business lending rate, has gone the way of the banker's green eyeshades. The prime rate has been so often misused, abused, and tortured in recent years that the phrase seems beyond repair.

I suggest that the tattered cloth of the prime rate not be rewoven but that a new phrase couched in simple language be adopted and hopefully adhered to faithfully by the commercial banking industry. Rather than painfully drawn qualifications about "prime", "LIBOR", "base", or other ersatz versions, I urge each bank to simply announce its *lowest* interest rate for business borrowers with all other business rates scaled upward from that rate. Thanks to the actions of

1. See footnote 5 to chapter 16 for the reference to the staff report.

the banking industry, the prime has little meaning today and it should be consigned to the junkyard for abused banking terms.

HON. FERNAND J. ST. GERMAIN
Chairman,
Committee on Banking,
Finance and Urban Affairs
United States House of Representatives
April, 1981

Congressman St. Germain's reference to a "base" rate should be familiar to Citibank borrowers. Citibank dropped the word "prime" several years ago. In 1984, Bank of America followed suit. Their "prime" is now called the "reference" rate, no doubt to convey the notion of a benchmark, but certainly not the lowest available rate.

Banks, of course, haven't tossed the phrase in the junkheap yet. They still use it and contend that it's set by market forces. Whether it is or not, it's important to realize that two popular notions about the prime rate are wrong. It's *not* set by the Fed. It's determined by each bank's top executives. And it's *not* the bank's basic rate for regular savings accounts. A study by the Hearst Corporation in 1983 found that approximately 33 percent of the public is laboring under this misconception.

With the freedom to set its own prime rate, a bank can choose its own position in the marketplace. A smaller bank might choose to make second-position real estate loans on apartment complexes at a time when few others are willing to do so. Such a bank will charge accordingly, for example, 3 points and 3 over prime. What the unsuspecting borrower might assume is that the prime rate being quoted is the prime you read or hear about. In fact, such a bank could be fixing its prime rate higher than the Bank of America's reference or Citibank's base rate. It is quoting and charging a prime rate decided by its own leadership. Even bankers, when they borrow for their personal needs, sometimes miss this point. I know this happens because one of my friends, a senior real estate loan officer, once made the following confession. He'd assumed that the rate he was paying was tied to a big-bank prime. Instead, the prime at the bank where he was borrowing was a ½ percent higher than his own bank's prime and higher than the big-bank prime reported in the press.

The first major point, then, is that the old, familiar definition is still familiar, but definitely not in use. If a bank is still using the word "prime," the definition in the promissory notes has probably been changed. The prime rate, by whatever name, is now just a number announced from time to time by the bank.

Perhaps one contribution of this book will be to point to the emperor and exclaim that he isn't wearing anything. The prime rate isn't really what the banks charge their best customers. Maybe that was true years ago. This definition holds no water today. Some major companies with strong financial statements borrow at rates below prime, while most borrow for more than prime. In truth, the prime rate is set at whatever rate will enable a bank, given its costs, to make money. And banks will lend at *any* rate which, in all mathematical simplicity, projects an acceptable yield.

The result is that the interest rate charged by the bank is truly up for negotiation. While the prime rate will always be referred to in these negotiations, there is nothing but "policy" which prevents a bank from striking any deal which attracts your business.[2]

So negotiate. The emperor hasn't a stitch.

2. Some banks, in order to avoid looking as though they're lending below prime, negotiate a below-prime rate for the loan, and then write the agreement so that the interest rate is tied to something else. One of the favorites is LIBOR, the London InterBank Overnight Rate.

CHAPTER 10

Five Below Prime

At this point, some of our basic observations should be reviewed.

One critical observation is that banks make money on demand deposits and, in fact, build their business-development efforts around attracting customers who have a strong ability to provide them with what they call "compensating balances." What we've learned is that banks manage their assets (i.e., loan portfolio) to achieve a desired ROA yield and, ultimately, an acceptable return on equity. You can easily determine a bank's asset to equity leverage by looking at the financial statements in the bank's lobby.

Another key observation concerns the realization that there is a cost if you're going to hold funds in checking rather than in savings accounts, but that you might be giving up less than you think because of the tax laws.

Finally, it is very important to realize that the prime rate only *seems* to be an impregnable barrier. If bankers describe it as such and we conduct ourselves accordingly, that societal "agreement" becomes firmly established. Since, in fact, this consensus already exists, it is only possible to break through it if we make banks compete for our business and show them why they can afford to engage in price competition that results in rates below prime.

In this chapter, I'll explain a basic concept that will remove all of the mystique about the banking business. In the next chapter, I'll explain the thinking behind a more precise approach.

When I first approached my bank on this basis, my theory was rough cut, to say the least. I had started from the premise that I had something that the bank didn't have, but wanted: money. I had some of it and one of my clients had some. My bank already had a relationship with me and so I could have started by threatening to go somewhere else. I chose the positive approach, however, and said that I could bring my client's deposits *to* the bank, not that I would take anything away. Since my client and I continually had the power to change banks at any time, the threat of withdrawing funds would be only to state the obvious and something which any customer can do on any given day. This was a power we couldn't lose. My client was an escrow company (see chapter 15) and the deposits were, for the most part, trust deposits which *didn't* earn interest and *couldn't* be pledged as collateral. It wasn't our money, but it had to be deposited in a bank. It's not necessary to *have* money if you *control* it.

My client and I had previously agreed that we were interested in acquiring other businesses in her field. Between us, we controlled approximately $600,000 in demand deposits. Between us, we owed short-term commercial loans of approximately $155,000. One loan had been fixed by her bank at 16 percent per annum. As prime went up, this loan looked better and better. As prime went down, it looked less attractive. Two other loans were at rates floating with the bank's prime rate. One loan, for $45,000, was secured by real estate and was priced at 2 percent over prime. Another loan of $30,000 was unsecured and priced at 2½ percent over prime. As the prime rate went up, these loans became very,

very expensive. Those of you who had such loans will remember the pain and the panic. When the prime rate averaged 20 percent during May through September of 1981, most of us were paying interest at the rate of 22 percent and 23 percent on our loans.

With our resources and our goals in mind, I asked the following question: if we maintained demand deposits of at least $400,000, would the bank rewrite our $155,000 in loans to 6 percent *below* prime on a floating basis, and give us a credit line of another $145,000 at the same rate (6 percent *below* prime), as well as *give* us computer services worth approximately $10,000 to meet my client's usual needs? Because our combined demand deposits fluctuated, we promised only a minimum of $400,000, reserving a cushion of $200,000. In return, we wanted to borrow $300,000 at 6 *below* prime.

I strongly believed that the bank could afford to make this agreement. This was the right question because it forced the analysis into the familiar one of income and expense. Based on the income the bank could anticipate from our deposit relationship, the deal was rewarding for both sides. I have to admit that it was brash to propose a below prime deal, and outrageous to propose anything like *6* percent below prime.

But I had my theory. So when the regional vice-president and assistant vice-president for commercial loans heard me out, they were listening not only to my proposal, but to my justification. At the time, the prime rate was 16½ percent. I also assumed (wrongly) that the reserve requirement was 25 percent, and I argued that demand deposits of $400,-000 would allow the bank to borrow $1,600,000 because of the reserve requirement leverage. This might cost them 12 percent if they used their own internal measure of their cost of funds (the thirty-day C.D. rate, they said) or perhaps less if they borrowed from the Federal Reserve. They could easily expect to find borrowers willing to pay, hypothetically, 2 over prime, or 18½ percent. The spread between 18 percent and 12 percent was 6½ percent. The projected annual interest income to the bank was $1,600,000 \times 6\frac{1}{2}$ percent, or $104,000.

This set the stage. We wanted to borrow $300,000 at 6 percent below prime, or at $10\frac{1}{2}$ percent, a loss to the bank of $1\frac{1}{2}$ percent as measured by their own cost of funds. This loss was an expense of the transaction equal to $300,000 \times 1\frac{1}{2}$ percent, or $4,500.

In addition to this loss-of-interest expense, we asked the bank to provide certain accounting services valued at $10,000.

On a crude basis then, the transaction could be summed up as follows:

Interest income to the bank		$104,000
Less: Loss on interest	$4,500	
Accounting services	10,000	
Transaction expense		$ 14,500
Net transaction income to bank		$ 89,500

With this admittedly cockeyed idea of the value of the relationship we proposed, we could now calculate a yield on the loans we wanted. Based on our assessment of the bank's income and expenses, the bank would earn $89,500 on the $300,000 in loans to be made. This was an ROA yield to the bank of $89,500 divided by $300,000, or 29.8 percent! Even though the assumptions were raw, the yield was high enough to justify our request.

Or so I said as matter of factly as I could. I was indeed in uncharted waters and afraid of being laughed out of the office. The theory seemed valid, the yield seemed high, and I knew that the simple calculations were correct.

But were the assumptions close enough to my banker's view of financial reality? Had I tapped into *his* paradigm of thinking about the value of demand deposits and the value of the relationship I was proposing?

He didn't immediately say "no." If I had totally missed the mark, I would have expected him to end the discussion immediately. Instead, he told us that he and his assistant vice-president would review our request and that we would meet again soon.

There was hope.

When we did meet again, the discussion was brief. He told me that 6 percent below prime was not something the bank could afford to do. I slumped. However (this was a very big word at the time), the bank *could* afford 5 below prime. Would we be willing to work out the details with his assistant vice-president? Although I was careful not to fall off my chair, I was mentally on cloud nine.

The point of this discussion is that my concept was right, although the theory on which my calculations were based was far from correct. The breakthrough was that banks are businesses first, and banks second. Just like us, they think in terms of income and expense, net income, and yield. What I learned from this first negotiation was that everything I was to the bank, as borrower, depositor, and recipient of services, could be quantified into an expected net income to the bank.

Income and expense. That's the conceptual bottom line.

CHAPTER 11

Other Deal Points

Let me highlight some of the details of my first negotiation. Nothing as dramatic as borrowing at 5 percent below prime is all that simple.

First, and perhaps as dramatic as the low rate itself, the agreement did not involve borrowing against cash. Borrowing against cash means putting the bank in the position of having cash as collateral. With cash as collateral, bankers have a lien on your money, whether interest bearing or not, in the event that you fail to repay a loan (a default). This lien right allows the bank to immediately apply the available cash to any unpaid loan which the bank calls because of a default. In our case, because we were working with non-interest-bearing trust deposits, the bank had no lien rights. The money belonged to somebody else. The bank made an underwriting decision that we could be trusted to repay the loans, and then it favorably priced the loans solely on account of the value of the business relationship we had to offer.

The reason this was such an important ingredient is

that, because of it, we maintained our independence. We wanted the bank to know at all times that we were free to move our valuable accounts elsewhere.

Of course, there were other aspects to consider as well. The rate was unbelievably low and, as you might well imagine, the agreement was fragile. Our deposits would be frequently monitored; the reins tightly held.

For example, the balances and rate were to be reviewed every quarter. If our balances were sufficient ($400,000 or above), the rate would remain at 5 percent below prime and the term would be renewed (rolled over) for the next ninety days. The rate would remain fixed for this period. If our balances were deficient, there was a penalty and we would be charged a "normal" rate of 2 percent over prime, but only on the shortfall.

There were two formulations of this downside penalty, but neither of them would have meant paying 2 over prime on our entire unpaid loan principal. Instead, in either formulation, we were to pay 2 percent over prime only on a *pro rata* basis. But there were two ways to figure that pro-rated amount. Let's say that our demand deposits were only $300,-000 instead of $400,000. The bank wanted to obligate us to pay 2 over prime on $100,000, which would be 33⅓ percent of our $300,000 in loans. However, since such a shortfall was only a 25 percent drop in the deposit relationship we promised, we proposed that the penalty be paid on $75,000, which would be 25 percent of our $300,000 in loans.

In the end, and because we had a $200,000 cushion in our anticipated deposit relationship, we agreed to the bank's formulation. Since the bank was willing to give us the benefits of a super rate, we had to be willing to bear a slight penalty if we failed to keep our end of the bargain.

In addition, the bank at first wanted to impose a maximum and minimum on the rate. The bank wanted our rate to float no lower than 8 percent (i.e., when the prime would be at 13 percent) and no higher than 20 percent (when the prime would be at 25 percent). If the prime moved to 11 percent, for example, our rate would be only 3 percent below prime. If the prime moved to 27 percent, we'd be 7 percent under. Later, for reasons the bank did not disclose, they removed these parameters. If the prime moved to 10 percent (which it approached in March of 1983), we'd pay 5 percent. Obviously, the bank had little doubt that the prime rate would both remain relatively high and continue to fluctuate.

Another important aspect was the agreement on repaying the principal. There were two formulations for this as well because we had two kinds of loans. The first loans we discussed were our existing loans of $155,000 which were, except for $30,000, secured by real estate. In addition to being collateralized, these loans had been made previously. It's always a little easier to make a loan that another banker had previously decided to make. Because of these factors, we asked for and won the right to repay principal over a ten-year (120-month) term. Thus, in addition to paying the interest portion on a monthly basis, we had to repay slightly less than 1 percent per month of the money we'd borrowed. To be precise, we had to pay interest on unpaid principal at 5 percent below prime, plus .0083333 of the original unpaid balance. Even if the rate changed, and we had to pay 2 percent over prime on a portion, the ten-year amortization schedule for *principal* would remain the same.

The second type of loan was the standing credit line of $145,000 for leasehold improvements and business acquisition purposes. Most acquisition loans have a short repayment schedule because they are associated with a relatively high risk. There is always more risk in doing something new. Usually the outer limit for the term of a business acquisition loan is five years. Even at 5 percent below prime, there was still room for negotiation in the transaction, and the bank accepted a five-year (60-month) repayment period. In other words, any funds we borrowed for business acquisition purposes would bear interest at the rate of 5 percent below prime, paid monthly, and we would make a monthly principal payment equal to 1/60th of the original principal amount.

In exchange for having the more favorable repayment

schedule, and because we wanted the bank as an ally and advisor, we also agreed to obtain the bank's prior consent for any acquisition we planned. Before we could draw on our credit line, the assistant vice-president would have to be convinced that the purchase made sense. We didn't at all mind having an intelligent third party review our plans because we knew that the mere preparation for such a presentation would disclose information gaps and unfavorable aspects. Besides, the assistant vice-president was bright and we valued her opinion.

In addition to the major features of the loan agreement, there was a laundry list of other conditions. You may well run into the following kinds of details:

A. Warranties and representations that
1. the documents were validly signed and delivered;
2. that all financial statements and data submitted to the bank were true and correct and that there were no materially adverse changes after the date shown on the statements;
3. that we were not a party to any litigation which was not disclosed; and
4. that there was no delinquency for any local, state, or federal taxes.

B. Agreements to
1. maintain property, equipment, and facilities in good order;
2. conduct business in a normal fashion without voluntary interruption;
3. maintain all insurance required by law or by agreements with lenders or landlords;
4. pay, before penalties accrue, all taxes, assessments, or other liabilities on property unless they were being contested in good faith, without a materially adverse effect, and if reserves had been set aside to pay if the contest was unfavorably resolved;
5. maintain a standard system of accounting in accord-

ance with generally accepted accounting principles, consistently maintained;

6. allow access by the bank's representatives to books and records at all reasonable times;

7. furnish financial statements internally prepared (i.e., unaudited) every six months;

8. furnish and certify a balance sheet and profit-and-loss (income) statement for each fiscal year prepared in accordance with generally accepted accounting principles;

9. certify in writing that each and every covenant in the loan agreement had been observed and performed and that no event had occurred and no condition existed which would constitute a default;

10. provide any other information that the bank might reasonably request from time to time;

11. not incur any other indebtedness other than in the ordinary course of business (i.e., for revolving credit agreements); and

12. not sell, lease, assign, or transfer all or substantially all of our assets without the bank's prior knowledge.

In other words, there was unquestionably a substantial burden to go along with a substantial benefit. Any business relationship as complex as a significant borrower/lender relationship with unusual terms may involve a veritable Christmas tree of custom provisions designed to protect both sides. While it was a struggle to wade through the legal thicket of provisions, the end result was very worthwhile.

Before I close this chapter, I have to stress that these other requirements are not always imposed. In 1983, when I refinanced my home, a car, my word-processor, and bought a business and an office building largely with borrowed funds at 4 percent below prime from a different (and much larger) bank (again, with no points), *none* of these provisions were imposed. And I was borrowing at no points and prime minus 4! As far as I'm concerned, however, always function as if these provisions applied. Because I feel this way about my "total relationship," and conduct myself accordingly, my banker is an ally, not an adversary.

I should also mention that the $300,000 loan package (the subject of my initial 5 percent below prime negotiation), even after complete documentation, was never finalized. When the branch manager of my client's then bank found out that he was about to lose the account, and what the terms were, he obtained approval from his chairman and the loan committee within a matter of days and offered 5 percent below prime *fixed for the rest of the year*. Now there was no reason to change banks.

How interesting, I said to myself. One bank was offering 5 percent below prime and another was actually writing a loan that way.

CHAPTER 12

Yield:

The Sophisticated Approach

$\mathbf{A}$s I said in Chapter 10, my initial formulation of the bank's yield was erroneous. I also knew that the mathematics applied only to the single case of our having $400,000 in deposits and a loan request of $300,000. So I pressed the issue by asking how the bank would view the situation if we maintained larger deposits. Would we be able to borrow for an even lower rate or, perhaps, borrow more money at the same low rates?

The assistant vice-president explained that my request had indeed been a novel one and that the bank's financial executives had reviewed the calculations. Their view of the approach was more sophisticated, but conceptually the same.

First of all, the bank makes calculations based on "average collected balances," not the "average ledger balances" which we sometimes see on our bank statements. There is a difference between the two because the bank gives credit for deposits immediately, but may not receive the money from the forwarding institution (e.g., the bank on which the check is drawn) until after several days. This is called Float (which I'll refer to as F). Unfortunately, the bank has no such delay factor when it is asked to pay on a check you have written. Your account is immediately reduced. Thus, the average collected balance (ACB) is less than the average ledger balance (ALB). As a formula, this relationship can be expressed as

$$ACB = ALB - F.$$

The next level involves calculating what the bank calls "net balances" (NB). Net balances are arrived at by deducting the appropriate reserve requirements from the average collected balance. Banks can only make money with money they can put to use. Since reserves must be sent to the Fed or held as vault cash, they must be netted out. I'll use $R(c)$ for the checking account reserves and $R(s)$ for the savings account reserves.

Net balances are then equal to average collected balances minus the reserves. Mathematically, these steps are as follows:

$$NB = ALB - R(c) - R(s).$$
$$= ACB - F - R(c) - R(s).$$

At this point, we have calculated the net amount of our balances. Now we need to calculate the *earning power* of our balances. There is an easy method of doing so using the Fed funds rate, and I'll explain it in detail in the next chapter.

Assuming that we have a formulation which relates balances to income, we must add in other sources of income and subtract the expenses which the bank anticipates. In our negotiations, we asked the bank to provide, at no additional cost to us, a computerized accounting system which would track certain transactions. Since the bank estimated that it would cost approximately $10,000 to provide their computerized accounting system to us for a year, the cost of services was set at $10,000.

We also must subtract the bank's cost on our below prime loans. The bank's cost of funds is equal to the average interest expense incurred when it pays the public to bring in deposits. The loan to us is multiplied by this average rate.

The final step is to simply divide the net income by the total loans involved (referred to as L) and thereby determine the return on asset yield the bank can anticipate by granting our loan request, even if the rate it charges on those loans is below prime. The formula for the bank's yield is

$$ROA \text{ yield} = Net\ Income/L$$

What ROA yield tells your banker is how much net income your portion of the loan portfolio will generate. Remember that the success of the bank depends on how well this loan portfolio is managed. Since loans are receivables (assets) for a bank, the relevant measure of your total relationship is how much net income your banker can expect from the total assets deployed. If we know the desired ROA yield, and how a banker calculates it, we can solve for the loan rate! Regardless of prime.

CHAPTER 13

The Hurdle Pricer

N ow let's look at it from the bank's point of view and detail the core concept precisely. The core concept, you'll recall, is that the bank can make money on your deposits as well as your loans and that, if you can quantify the bank's income on the deposit side of the ledger, you can argue for a reduction in the cost of your loans. This looks like the proverbial rabbit-out-of-the-hat magic trick only because the banks have been absolutely great at the magician's art of diverting your attention. Once you see how it's done, you'll see it as being rather simple.

The "hurdle pricer" is one *banker's* form for making the same yield calculations that we made earlier. The hurdle pricer ("hurdler" for short) was given to me by a banker who was the executive vice-president in charge of his bank's commercial lending. He told me it was modeled on the Citibank form by the same name.[1] It's a step-by-step program for cal-

---

1. The Bank of America version is called a Spread Pricer. It's more difficult to use because everything is couched in terms of percent. The

culating the net revenue to be expected based on the *total relationship* (my favorite phrase). Other than some minor changes for clarity, what you'll see is what was handed to me over lunch.

There are three stages to the hurdler—income, expense, and profitability. Under "income," the hurdler asks for fill-ins to discern (1) the amount of interest to be earned on the requested loan, (2) the interest being earned on existing loans, (3) points or fees to be earned, *and* (4) earnings on balances.

Under "income," the hurdler involves thirteen steps:

 1. Requested Loan Amount   _____
 2. Rate _____
 3. Interest Earned on Requested Loan $ _____
 4. Average Balance of Existing Loan(s)   _____
 5. Average Rate _____
 6. Interest Earned on Existing Loan(s)   _____
 7. Average Total Loans   _____
 8. Annualized Fees   _____
 9. a. Average Collected Balances
       b. DDA _____   less 12% Reserve   _____
       c. Time _____   less   3% Reserve   _____
10. Net Balances   _____
11. Earnings Rate _____
       (Prior 30 days average Fed funds rate)
12. Earnings on Balances (Line 10 × 11)
13. Total Revenue $ _____

Notice, in the hurdler format, the bank used the "prior 30 days average Fed funds rate" to determine its earnings on balances. The Fed funds rate is a daily rate at which banks make overnight loans of balances in excess of reserve requirements to other banks. It's what bankers charge each

---

Hurdle Pricer is couched in terms of dollars and converted to a percentage figure for the ROA yield. B of A's 1980 Spread Pricing Guide for Domestic Commercial Loans gives an example of a desired net ROA yield of 1.45 percent. Because the bank's assets are assumed to be 20 times the bank's equity, the return-on-equity, or ROE, yield would be 29 percent (as a goal, of course).

other, not us. You and I know that the banks charge rates *over* prime to the vast majority of borrowers, excluding the banks who borrowed from them. So it's relatively conservative to calculate earnings on balances as if they commanded only the rate charged to other banks and not the rates charged to corporate and individual borrowers.

The second aspect of the hurdler is a five-step program listing expenses:

14. Cost of Funds _____ × Line 7
  (Average of current 30- and 90-day C.D. rates) $ ____
15. Cost of Interest-Earning Deposits ____
16. Service and Other Charges ____
17. Other Costs ____
18. Total Expenses $ ____

Finally, "loan profitability" is the simple summary of the simple multiplications, additions, and subtractions. The hurdle rate is a figure which estimates the bank's overhead, cost of risk and net ROA yield, and thus it becomes the figure to beat, the hurdle to overcome. If you do overcome it, the bank considers the loan to be profitable. In our calculations, my banker friend specified 5 percent as the hurdle rate. The hurdle rate was composed of three parts: overhead, cost of risk, and net ROA yield.

19. Net Income (Line 13 − Line 18) $ ____
20. Gross Yield % (Line 19 ÷ Line 7) ____ %
21. Hurdle Rate 5.0%
22. Over/(under) ____

Using the hurdle pricer, a banker can tell whether a loan will, at the requested rate, prove to be worth doing even assuming a below prime rate on the loan. Let's work through an example. Suppose prime is 11 percent, the Fed funds rate is 8.8 percent, and the bank's cost of funds is 9 percent. It may seem strange, looking at this example, that the bank can make money with a hypothetical earning rate of only 8.8 percent against a cost of funds of 9.0 percent. To understand this apparent anomaly, you need only recall that the bank is making money in two places—on the loans and on the balances.

The example (Figure 13–1) is based on my request to borrow $30,000 at 2 percent below prime (i.e. 9 percent) with no points. I was offering $50,000 in a 5¼ percent sav-

Borrower Name:		Loan Commitment:	$
Loan Type:	New:	Renewal	
Related Borrowers:		Officer:	
Account Name:		Date:	

Income

1. Requested Loan Amount	30,000		
2. Rate	9.0%		
3. Interest Earned on Requested Loan		$2,700	
4. Average Balance of Existing Loans	N/A		
5. Average Rate			
6. Interest Earned on Existing Loan(s)		N/A	
7. Average Total Loans	30,000		
8. Annualized Fees		N/A	
9. Average Collected Balances	50,000		
DDA N/A Less 12% Reserve	N/A		
Time $50,000 Less 3% Reserve	48,500		
10. Net Balances	48,500		
11. Earnings Rate	8.8%		
(Prior 30 days average Fed funds rate)			
12. Earnings on Balances (Line 10 × 11)		4,268	
13. Total Revenue		$6,968	

Expenses

14.	Cost of Funds: 9.0% × line 7	$2,700
	(average of current 30 + 90 day C.D. Rates)	
15.	Cost of Interest-Earning Deposits	
	($50,000 × .0525)	2,625
16.	Service and activity charges	N/A
17.	Other Costs	N/A
18.	Total Expenses	$5,325

Loan Profitability

19.	Net Income (Line 13 − Line 18)	$1,643
20.	Gross Yield % (Line 19 ÷ Line 7)	5.48%
21.	Hurdle Rate	5.0%
22.	Over/(under)	.48%

Fig. 13–1. Hurdle Pricer Example.

ings account. I had to beat a hurdle rate of 5 percent and, as you can see, I did so. If I had been working with an interest-free checking account, the results would have been even more dramatic.

The blank hurdle pricer is shown in Fig. 13–2. I've supplied a blank form so that you can experiment with the balances and rates out of your own experience.

The hurdle pricer handed to me by my banker specified a hurdle rate of 5 percent. This is *not* the same thing as a return on asset (ROA) yield. The 5 percent figure, the banker explained, is composed of the following: 3 percent for general overhead, 1 percent for cost of risk, and only *1 percent* for *net* return on asset yield.

While I thought at first that a 1 percent net ROA yield looked very skimpy, I thought differently after I realized that banks were built on leverage. A 1 percent ROA yield might turn out to be 20 percent return on equity, the real bottom line depending on the bank's own leverage.

In fact, a 1 percent ROA yield, net, is considered healthy. For example, in the March 21, 1984, issue of *Business*

Week, only 40 banks out of the largest 150 had ROA yields of 1.00 or better in 1982. The average ROA yield was only .76 percent for the 150 largest banks; the highest was 1.50 percent.

So, in order to compare apples to apples, it is vital to understand the exact nature of the goal. Is it net ROA yield?

Borrower Name:	Loan Commitment: $

Loan Type:	New:	Renewal

Related Borrowers:	Officer:

Account Name:	Date:

Income

  1. Requested Loan Amount   _____
  2. Rate   _____
  3. Interest Earned on Requested Loan $ _____
  4. Average Balance of Existing Loans   _____
  5. Average Rate   _____
  6. Interest Earned on Existing Loan(s)   _____
  7. Average Total Loans   _____
  8. Annualized Fees   _____
  9. Average Collected Balances   _____
      DDA _____ Less 12%
      Reserve   _____
      Time _____ Less 3%
      Reserve   _____
10. Net Balances   _____
11. Earnings Rate   _____
    (Prior 30 days average Fed funds rate)
12. Earnings on Balances (Line 10 × 11)   _____
13. Total Revenue $ _____

Expenses

14. Cost of Funds: ____ × line 7 $ _____
    (average of current 30 + 90 day C.D.
    Rates)
15. Cost of Interest-Earning Deposits   _____
    (calculate separately)
16. Service and Activity Charges   _____
17. Other Costs   _____
18. Total Expenses $ _____

Loan Profitability

19. Net Income (Line 13 − Line 18) $ _____
20. Gross Yield % (Line 19 ÷ Line 7)   ____ %
21. Hurdle Rate   ____ %
22. Over/(under)   _____

Fig. 13-2. Hurdle Pricer Format.

Is it an ROA yield which is, in some way, a gross yield? Is it a
"hurdle rate" designed to cover ROA yield, cost of risk and
overhead? This is the kind of shop talk you need to have with
your banker.

Here's an example of just what I mean. The hurdle
pricer was, as I say, handed to me by a banker. While it may
have been modeled after the Citibank version, my banker
was using it in the context of a bank with less than $100 mil-
lion in assets, a small bank. I was delighted to discover a
variation on the theme when I was talking with a loan officer
working for one of the nation's largest 20 banks. Their version was different in some respects, but very similar (see Figure 13-3).

Notice, for example, that some of the terminology is different, but that the relationship is cast in terms of income
and expense. Notice that "Pre-Tax Contribution" is the result of subtracting Line 12 ("Total Expenses") from Line 6
("Gross Income"). Pre-Tax Contribution is our old friend,
net income. Notice, too, that "Contribution on Assets" is the
result of dividing Line 13 (Pre-Tax Contribution or net in-

come) by "E" (Average Loan Outstanding). This is another friend, return on asset (ROA) yield.

This worksheet, which doesn't have a name, really locked things down for me. There might be variations to pricing, but they are only that. In this particular case, I think you can see that the worksheet differs from the hurdle pricer in that there are two additional expense line items: Cost of Risk and Loan Handling Costs. Because of these ex-

---

Profitability Data

A) Average Ledger Balance _____
B) Average Collected Balance _____
C) Average Residual Balance _____
D) Average Commitment _____
E) Average Loan Outstanding _____
F) Net Funds Used (Supplied) _____
    Customer Since _____
    Credit Rating _____
G) Percentage Residual Balance/
    Loan Balance _____
H) Pool Funds Rate
    (Est. Avg. for Term of Loan) _____
I) Prime/Pool Spread
    (Est. Avg. Prime − H) _____
J) Spread over Cost of Funds
    (I + Spread over Prime) _____
K) Average Rate on Loan O/S _____
    Zip Code _____
    S.I.C. _____

Income

1) Interest Earned (derived: $E \times K$) $ _____
2) Earnings on Deposits
    ((B − Res. Req.) $\times$ H) _____
3) Fees in Lieu of Balances (Earned) _____
4) Commitment Fees _____
5) Other income _____
6) Gross Income $ _____

Expense

7) Cost of Funds (E × H) $ _____
8) Cost of Risk (Line E × .30%)
   (% Fluctuates with Risk Class & Collateral)   _____
9) Loan Handling Costs
   (% Varies with Loan Type)
         Fixed   (Line E × 1.0%)   _____
         Variable (Line E × .48%)   _____
10) Deposit Activity Charges   _____
11) Interest Paid on Deposits   _____
12) Total Expenses $ _____
13) Pre-Tax Contribution
   (Line 6 less Line 12) $ _____

| | | Increases Needed to Meet Goal | |
	Goal	Rate	Balances
Contribution on Assets (Line 13 divided by E)	1.5%		

Fig. 13–3. Hurdle Pricer Variation.

penses, the net income derived from the total relationship will be lower. While a lower net income will lead to a lower ROA yield, that's less of a problem than you might think. Since we've already considered cost of risk and a major overhead item, loan handling costs, the ROA yield will be nearer to an ROA yield net of all costs. I asked my friend what sort of goal yield he was looking for. More shop talk. I was concerned that the added expenses in this worksheet would make it hard to hit the target of a 5 percent ROA yield. He told me, to my great relief, that *his* bank sought an ROA yield of 1.5 percent, and that this was a better deal than the bank he used to work for (another large, top 20 bank), which wanted an ROA yield of 1.65 percent.

It should also be clear now why a banker's not crazy to make below prime loans to me. The loan interest rate is only a component of the ROA calculation. My approach is to set the mix of deposits, loans, and interest rates which will result in the bank's desired ROA yield. Banks certainly aren't loaning me money at 4 percent below prime for the privilege of losing money. I'm profitable for them, and they'd like to have more of me.

For you and for me, the lesson is clear. Find out how your banker thinks about pricing. Ask him or her to explain their "hurdler," "worksheet," "pricer," or whatever they call it. Learn the elements of the calculation and discover the bank's yield goal. Then use all of the information available to you concerning your deposits, your loan needs, the interest you desire to earn on your balances, the bank's cost of funds, and so on, and calculate *backwards* to find the loan rate which will give the bank the yield it wants in the first place. I do this now with a modifiable microcomputer program I developed which I call LoanRate. Have IBM; will travel.

CHAPTER 14

Proof of the Pudding

If you'll reflect on the hurdle pricer for a moment, you might find it mind-boggling to realize that prime is irrelevant to the calculations. After setting the ROA yield and solving for the loan interest rate which will achieve it, the result is compared to prime. Prime comes into the picture only at this point, when the work's all done. For example, you might require that your deposits earn some specific amount of interest (thus increasing expenses), and see what happens to the loan rate. Only then do you compare the result to prime.

It may seem funny, and require some getting used to, but the truth is that the prime rate is really only relevant when it comes to writing up the loan documents. Then, by convention, the loan interest rate is tied to prime. If the loan interest rate turns out to be 11 percent when prime is 16 percent, then the loan might be written at 5 percent "below" prime (see Fig. 14-1 (Bank A), 1982). If the simple calculations lead to a loan interest rate of 8 percent while prime is 12 percent, then the notes can be written as 4 percent "less than" prime (see Figs. 14-2a, 14-2b, 14-2c and 14-2d (Bank B), 1983; and Fig. 14-3 (Bank C), 1984).

See? I wasn't kidding.

On demand, or if no demand, on _____

_____ , or order, at its _____

_____ Office in the City of _____ Los Angeles _____

* * *THIRTY-SEVEN THOUSAND FIVE HUNDRED AND NO/100* * * *FIVE*

___ January 5, 1982 ___ at the rate of * * *FIVE*

with interest on unpaid principal from ___ below ~~xxxxxx~~ the prime rate of interest which the Bank charges corporate borrowers of

___ 5.00 ___%) per annum ~~xxxxx~~ the prime rate may change from time to time. Any changes in said prime rate shall become short-term unsecured loans, which rate may change in said prime rate. Interest is computed hereunder on the basis of a 360-day year and effective date of the change in said prime rate. Interest is computed hereunder ___ February 4 ___ , 19 82 . There is a minimum inter

payable ___ at maturity ___ , beginning ___ February 4 ___ , 19 82 . There is a minimum inter

payable ___ at maturity ___ , then after maturity, any principal remaining outstanding shall bear interest a at maturity, any principal remaining outstanding shall also be computed on the b

After demand, or if no demand, then after maturity, at the interest rate specified above, which interest shall also be computed on the b percent (5%) per annum higher than the interest rate specified above, which interest shall also be computed on the b days elapsed. Principal and interest payable in lawful money of the United States.

The makers, sureties, endorsers, and guarantors hereof, agree: (1) to pay all cost of collection, including reasonal collection of this note; (2) to renewals and extensions of time at or after the maturity hereof; (3) to waive diligen protest, demand, and notice of dishonor; (4) to waive the right to plead any statute of limitations as a defense to any with any security herefor to the full extent permitted by law; (5) that no failure on the part of the holder of this r privilege hereunder, or to insist upon prompt compliance with the terms hereof, shall constitute a waiver thereof.

_____

Fig. 14-1. 1982 Unsecured Loan from Bank A.

MATURITY DATE: 10-01-84

ACCOUNT N[...]

...LSON E. Jt/w LOIS M.

Los Angeles _____ , California   Date ___ September 29, 198[...]

maker(s) promise(s) to pay to _____

or order, at its _____   In instalments, at the tim[...]

the principal sum of ___ SIX THOUSAND TWO HUNDRED and NO/100 _____

together with interest from date on the unpaid principal at the rate set forth below, or $ 100.00

    at the rate of ___ n/a ___ % per year,

    at the rate of ___ 4.00 ___ % per year, ~~higher than~~ less than

as its Prime Rate, and which shall vary concurrently with any change in such rate. , Prime Rate of Interest which is that rate ann[...]

Interest shall be computed at the above rate on the basis of the actual number of days during which the principal hereunde[...]
the purposes of this note, be one year.

Interest shall be payable ___ with each principal instalment _____

rincipal shall be payable in instalments of ___ ONE HUNDRED SEVENTY THREE and NO/100 _____ , and if [...]
173.00 _____), or more, each instalm---

inning ___ November 1 ___

Fig. 14-2a. 1983 Equipment Loan from Bank B.

_____, California   Date **September 29, 1983**

maker(s) promise(s) to pay to

the principal sum of _____ or order, at its _____

together with interest from date, on the unpaid principal at the rate set forth below, or $ **100.00**

EIGHT THOUSAND AND NO/100

In instalments, at the times

☐   at the rate of **n/a** % per year,
☒   at the rate of **4.00** % per year, Less than ~~XXXXX~~

as its Prime Rate, and which shall vary concurrently with any change in such rate.

Prime Rate of Interest which is that rate annou

terest shall be computed at the above rate on the basis of the actual number of days during which the principal hereunder i

: purposes of this note, be one year.

erest shall be payable _____ **with each principal instalment**

cipal shall be payable in instalments of _____ **TWO HUNDRED TWENTY-THREE AND NO/100** _____, and if n

223.00 _____), or more, each instalment due on the _____ **19th** _____ day of each

ning **October 19** , 19 **83** . On **September 19** , 19 **84** , all principal

lefault, the whole sum of principal and interest shall

aker(s) to pay in

Fig. 14–2b. 1983 Car Loan from Bank B.

NOTE SECURED BY DEED OF TRUST
(FLOATING RATE NOTE)

$ 45,000.00

Los Angeles _____, California __September 26,__

(City)

On __October 1__ , 19 84 _____

verally, promise(s) to pay to the order of _____ for value received, the un

this city, or at such other place as the holder of this note may from time to time designate in writing,

__FORTY FIVE THOUSAND and NO/100__ _____ at its office at

gether with interest from date hereof computed on principal balances hereof from time to time outsta

the rate which is __FOUR__ _____ percent (4.00 %) per year XXXXXXXX less than

erest which is that rate announced by the Bank at its Corporate Headquarters as its Prime Rate, and

rently with any change in such rate.

Interest XXXXXXXXXXXXXXXXXXXXXXXXXXXXXXXXXXXXXXXXXXXXXXXXXXX

XXXXXXXXXXXXXXXXXXXXXXXXXXXXXXXXXXXXXXXXXXXXXXXXXXXXXXXXXXXXXX

multiplying the then outstanding principal balance by 1/360th of the above annual interest rateXXXXXX shall

XXXXXXXXXXXXXXXXXXXXXXXXXXXXXXXXXXXXXXXXXXXXXXXXXXXXXXXXXXXXXX

:erest shall be payable with each principal instalment, and if not so

:ome part of the principal.

ncipal shall be payable in instalments of $____

more each instalment.

Fig. 14-2c. 1983 Second-Position Home Loan from Bank B.

79

———————, California   Date September 28, 198__

maker(s) promise(s) to pay to ———————, or order, at its ———————

In instalments, at the tim__

the principal sum of   ONE HUNDRED TWENTY FIVE THOUSAND and NO/100

together with interest from date on the unpaid principal at the rate set forth below, or $ 100.00

[ ] at the rate of   n/a   % per year,

[X] at the rate of   4.00   % per year, less than PERCENT

as its Prime Rate, and which shall vary concurrently with any change in such rate.   Prime Rate of Interest which is that rate an__

Interest shall be computed at the above rate on the basis of the actual number of days during which the principal hereunde__

the purposes of this note, be one year.

Interest shall be payable   with each principal instalment

Principal shall be payable in instalments of   TWO THOUSAND EIGHTY FOUR and NO/100

2,084.00   ), or more, each instalment due on the   1st   day of each __ , and if

beginning   November 1 , 19 83 . On   October 1 , 19 84 , all principal and i__

In default, the whole sum of principal and interest shall become due __

e maker(s) to pay interest or principal __ __

llectively __ __

Fig. 14-2d. 1983 Unsecured Loan from Bank B.

BORROWER NAME	SOCIAL SECURITY NUMBER	MATURITY DATE	BORROWER NO.	NOTE NUMBER
BRESTOFF, NELSON		04-02-85	001-049744	U0390

LOS ANGELES _____, California   Date ____OCTOBER 2, 1984_____ $ ___50,000.00- - - -

ON DEMAND OR IF NO DEMAND IS MADE THEN ON 4-2-85- - - - - _____ after date, for value received, the undersigned

maker(s) promise(s) to pay to _____, or order, at its   HEADQUARTERS _____, Office,

the principal sum of - - - - - -FIFTY THOUSAND AND NO/100- - - - - - - - - - - - DOLLARS,
together with interest from date on the unpaid principal hereof:

☐ at the rate _____ % per year, less than

☒ at the rate of -4.0- - - - % per year XXXXXXX of the prime rate of interest which ____ Bank charges,
which shall vary concurrently with any change in such prime rate, or $ ___-20,000- ____, whichever is greater. The prime rate
is that rate publicly announced by ____ Bank as its prime rate. Interest shall be computed at the above rate on the basis of the
actual number of days during which the principal hereunder is outstanding divided by 365 which shall, for the purposes of this note, be one year.
Interest shall be payable:

☒ monthly   ☐ quarterly   ☐ _____ beginning 11-02-84, and if not so paid shall become part of the principal.

Upon default, the whole sum of principal and interest shall become due immediately at the option of the holder hereof. Default shall include, but not be limited to, the failure of the maker(s) to pay interest or principal when due; the filing as to each person obligated hereon, whether as maker, co-maker, endorser or guarantor (hereafter individually or collectively referred to as the "Obligor") of a voluntary or involuntary petition under the provisions of the Federal Bankruptcy Act, the issuance of any attachment or execution against any material asset of any Obligor; default by any Obligor on any obligation concerning the borrowing of money; the death of any Obligor; or any deterioration of the financial condition of any Obligor which results in the holder hereof deeming itself, in good faith, insecure.

In the event of default, at the option of the holder hereof, interest may be charged on the amount delinquent at a rate 8% greater than the interest rate contracted for on the principal herein, effective from the date that such amount(s) shall become overdue, and the day following any other event of default. Such increased rate of interest shall continue until such delinquent amount(s), with interest thereon at the increased rate, shall have been paid or such other event of default has been cured to the satisfaction of the holder hereof.

If this note is not paid when due, each Obligor promises to pay all costs and expenses of collection and reasonable attorneys' fees incurred by the holder hereof on account of such collection, whether or not suit is filed thereon. Each Obligor shall be jointly and severally liable hereon and consents to renewals, replacements, and extensions of time for payment hereof, before, at, or after maturity; consents to the acceptance, release, or substitution of security for this note; and waives demand and protest and the right to assert any statute of limitations. Each Obligor waives the right, if any, to the benefit of, or to direct application of, any security hypothecated to the holder hereof until all indebtedness of the maker(s) to the holder hereof has been paid. Each Obligor waives the right, if any, to require the holder hereof to proceed against the maker(s) or to pursue any other remedy in its power; and agrees that the holder hereof may proceed against any one or more of the Obligors directly and independently of the maker(s), and that the cessation of the liability of the maker(s) for any reason other than full payment shall not affect the liability of each Obligor. Any married person who signs this instrument agrees that recourse may be had against his/her separate property for any obligations hereunder. The indebtedness evidenced hereby shall be payable in lawful money of the United States. In any action brought under or arising out of this note, each Obligor, including his/her successor(s) or assign(s), hereby consents to the jurisdiction of any competent court within the State of California, and consents to service of process by any means authorized by California Law.

X___Nelson Brestoff___
NELSON BRESTOFF

Payment Guaranteed by: _____

N-112 (5/83) Financial Suppliers

Fig. 14–3. 1984 Unsecured Loan from Bank C.

CHAPTER 15

Where the Money Is

Although my own negotiations have sometimes involved hundreds of thousands of dollars, it's clear that the bank's yield is not at all a function of how much money is involved. What counts is the mix of deposits, loans, and interest rates relative to each other.

However, it is fairly obvious that a banker will tend to be much more inclined to make below-prime loans if the borrower can offer, in one sitting, a significant deposit relationship. These deposit/loan relationships involve a banker's personal attention. Such handling, as opposed to the usual computer monitoring, is expensive, and a banker is only going to be willing to give your proposal such personal attention if there's enough money involved. One banker told me that you'll need to have or control about $25,000 before you can turn any heads.

With this in mind, and with the knowledge that the deposit relationship is a powerful one, a natural next step is to investigate how to obtain control of more money.

Usually, the control of money involves ownership or exclusive possession. But there are a number of ways and a number of businesses in which a great deal of money is controlled (not to mention banking) without ownership or exclusive possession. Let's take a look at just a few of them, noting in advance that they all involve some form of stewardship.

One of the most obvious examples whereby someone controls the money of another is the executorship or conservatorship. In these cases, someone is chosen to marshall the assets and liabilities of someone who has passed away or is otherwise incapable of dealing with their business affairs. For my example, I'm also going to assume that the executor will also ultimately be the sole heir.

Unfortunately, the winding up of an estate is a time-consuming process. As an heir, you may be unable to obtain the distribution of proceeds to which you have a justifiable expectation. In the event that you have a need for money, you might apply to your banker for a loan, as you would have if you needed to borrow against a C.D. Unfortunately, the money you stand to inherit, because it still belongs to the estate, is completely unavailable to serve as collateral. This situation is simply not the same as when you were willing to pledge your own funds as the source of repayment. In order to borrow at reduced rates, you must approach your banker with a loan-pricing theory which reflects the thinking we have outlined. You can do it because, as executor, you control the estate accounts.

Now there is a caution to this. As an executor, you have certain fiduciary responsibilities. Suppose there are other heirs. They and the court that appointed you will expect that you take some reasonable action to earn interest on the money in your control. You cannot prejudice the affairs of the estate in order to benefit yourself. For any significant financial transaction or strategy, you would be wise to obtain advance written consent for your plans. You must always be aware, especially when others are financially interested, that you may have a duty to act as any prudent person would act if he or she were investing for their own account. But the important thing to keep in mind here is that, for a short period of time, you're more important to your banker not because you might inherit some money, but because you *control* the money belonging to the estate.

Let's take a few more examples. In recent days, bankruptcies have occurred far more frequently than before. In a bankruptcy estate, a trustee acts very much like an executor, marshalling assets and applying them to liabilities. In the meantime, however, the trustee in bankruptcy is in control of the assets, including cash. Because there have been more bankruptcies recently, there's more cash involved now than ever before. In response, some banks have set up special departments to cater to trustees and, of course, the deposits they control. Now you know why.

Several other examples of money control come to mind from the real estate field: property management, escrow, and the title insurance business. In property management, whether of commercial or residential income property, the tenants usually pay a security deposit of some kind. The deposit, in whatever amount, can cover such items as rent, cleaning charges, expenses for repairs above normal wear and tear, and so on. At the end of the tenancy, the owner generally will be required to account for the deposit by showing how it was used and by returning the balance, if any. In the meantime, it is usually the case that the deposit is paid in at the beginning of the term and is held by the owner (or property manager) "interest-free." While such an owner might want to earn interest on these deposits, he or she might be better off holding them in a checking account and borrowing at more favorable rates. In any case, the deposits, while still technically belonging to the tenant, are in the control of the owner or manager.

A perfect example from the real estate field is the escrow. An escrow company acts as a stakeholder and is otherwise neutral. The company simply follows instructions and delivers a deed only when it has been given the cash required to close the deal, all other conditions having been satisfied. In California, the escrow is prevalent. Throughout the country, however, this stakeholder responsibility is generally handled by a title insurance company or a real estate attorney. When an escrow is opened, it is normal for the buyer to make a "good faith" deposit of several thousand dollars. A $3,000 deposit would not be unusual in a deal involving several hundred thousand dollars. A $10,000 deposit would not be unusual in a deal involving a million dollars. Indeed, if the transaction is both substantial and complicated, the seller might bargain for additional deposits at specified stages. While such deposits can be held in interest-bearing accounts, with interest accruing in favor of the person making the deposit, the deposits for the typical escrow of a single family home are generally held in trust *checking* accounts, primarily because no one anticipates that the escrow will be open for more than thirty to sixty days. Obviously, an escrow company with a sizeable number of open escrows will control hundreds of thousands of dollars, if not millions. In an active market, even small companies might have millions in their trust checking account. For our purposes, this is high octane fuel because there's no expense to the bank. As a result, escrow companies are special favorites of the bankers. They actively solicit escrow companies and, most importantly, offer loans below prime to an owner who knows the true power of the company trust account.

In the title insurance field, the stakes are even higher. Title insurance companies often act as escrow holders in many states (e.g., Texas and Georgia). In addition to the trust deposits under the company's control as an escrow holder, however, the title insurance companies collect impounds for property taxes and fire and liability insurance. Impounds are advance payments which transfer control of the money before the taxes or premiums are actually due. While the profitability of an escrow company or title insurance company might depend on its reputation and efficiency in providing the services for which it earns fees and premiums, there is little doubt that one of the great financial boons to owning or controlling an escrow or title insurance business is that they inherently involve large deposits from other people to be held in trust checking accounts.

Still another example in the real estate field is the mortgage company or mortgage banker. There, money is earned primarily by borrowing at one rate and lending at another. When the money is lent, of course, there is a deed of trust or mortgage given as collateral, and invariably these security devices call for the payment of tax and insurance impounds. The lender insists on these payments so that their lending position is not undercut by a foreclosure due to nonpayment of taxes (the lien of which is superior to any deed of trust or mortgage) or a disaster. But just as obviously, the mortgage company or banker is paid these additional sums before the twice-a-year property taxes or once-a-year insurance premiums have to be paid.

While it holds these funds, the mortgagor is generally free to negotiate with them. Since the mortgage banker earns his or her money by borrowing for less and lending for more, these impounds for taxes and insurance are welcome indeed. In fact, if there is a field where borrowing below prime based on demand deposits is the rule rather than the exception, it's mortgage banking. It's these impounds which allow the mortgage banker to borrow below prime and create a very healthy lending spread.

In addition to the spread, however, the impounds provide the mortgage banker with yet another key to business success: the use of someone else's larger and more sophisticated computer. For example, the larger mortgage bankers work with their *bank's* computer for loan-servicing purposes. If an elaborate computer system had to be designed and implemented especially for the mortgage banker, mortgage banking would be absolutely no fun at all. So, the clever mortgage banker trades a portion of his deposit relationship for use of the bank's mainframe computers and the elaborate, expensive computer programs that go with them. While this kind of banking service is more than you might ever want from your bank, it illustrates my point. And, in addition to computer time, mortgage bankers use their deposit clout to get such things as payroll processing, deposit messenger service, and bookkeeping assistance.

How are the services priced? Well, if you're large

enough, you don't bother with pricing. You simply say to the two or three banks with whom you'd be willing to do business that you have $20 million in demand deposits and you want their best package of services along with a quote on their lowest interest rate for the level of credit you want.

If your level of deposits is much smaller, you can only price the services on a comparison basis. You need to know what a particular service might cost before you can evaluate the value the bank places on it. In my own experience, the bank's assistant vice-president talked with the person handling the in-house computerized accounting system and then quoted to me a "cost of services" figure of $10,000. Now, this is an estimated value only. Because the bank's system may have been underutilized, the actual cost to the bank may have been less.

A mortgage banker friend of mine handled his negotiations for both services and a low-rate credit line by putting the banks in cutthroat competition with each other. Of course, he was dealing with large numbers. After getting a quote from one bank, he simply asked the other one to meet it or do better. He relied on the assumption that the banks were competing for his valuable deposits and would sharpen their pencils by virtue of being shopped. This is the kind of horse trading which business people have been doing with "compensating balances."

The only weakness in this approach, in which you simply don't care how the bankers are adding things up, is that you can only hope that the best bottom-line offer represents the best that can be had. Perhaps I worry too much. I want to know a lot more about how the banker's thinking so that I can make a request that will start the competition at levels that the bankers, even when competing with each other, might never consider. From what I've said so far, it should be clear that any industry or service in which deposits or impounds are common is rife with opportunity. The astute businessman, large or small, has a stronger argument for a better banking relationship than he or she might have realized.

Let's come back down to earth. I realize that mortgage

banking may not be an easy example to grasp. There's another example that will make things clear. Many people have opened individual retirement accounts (IRAs) or, if they're in business for themselves, Keogh plans. Still others do business in a corporate format and use corporate pension plans. All of these plans involve setting aside money for a long period of time and the continual accrual of interest which isn't taxed until withdrawn. After a while even IRAs add up to big money. This money isn't currently available (there are penalties for early withdrawal), but it is within your control. Thus, while there may be an obligation to have these funds in high interest-bearing accounts, the money can be used to reduce the cost of your borrowings. They form a deposit base for which the banks actively compete.

CHAPTER 16

Selling Commercial Paper

There are usually more ways than one to accomplish the same result. Let's talk about the unfamiliar world of commercial paper. Sophisticated financial executives can sometimes use commercial paper to borrow below prime. Because the transactions are usually amongst large businesses and for millions of dollars, the subject hasn't exactly become dinner table conversation. And although you may never have occasion to sell commercial paper, you ought to understand how it's used.

Let's begin by comparing it to borrowing from a bank. When you borrow from a bank, you deliver your application, financial statement, tax returns, and promissory note to the bank and the bank delivers Federal Reserve Notes— money—to you. With commercial paper, the company needing cash approaches individuals or companies with temporary excesses of cash. Of course, this is done through a marketplace and there is usually no direct contact between the executive whose cup runneth over and the executive whose cupboard is bare. The company needing cash signs a contract to repay what's lent with interest within a short period of time. The person or company with extra cash lends it to obtain the interest.

Commercial paper is short-term financing and is lent for up to only 270 days at the longest. When the debt is due, the borrowing company engages in another round of selling commercial paper. The proceeds of the new are used to retire the paper of the old. This is called a "rollover."

Besides being short term, commercial paper is usually a high-quality instrument. There are rating services that grade the financial history and health of large businesses who want to sell commercial paper. The paper is rated "A," "AA," "AAA," and so on. An "A" rating is the highest and generally requires the company to have previously arranged for a backup line of credit with banks so that there is a second source of timely repayment. A company with strong balances might use some of them to obtain a line of credit with a bank in order to get the higher rating. The cost is not terribly high because the whole idea of a backup line of credit is to use it infrequently. Since half the cost of a line (in terms of balances) is based on usage, a backup line of credit ties up only half as much money in demand deposits as might otherwise be the case.

Now the reason a company wants to sell commercial paper is that the price paid for the use of the money can be 1 to 4 percent below the then-prevailing bank prime rate for loans. Since a company with a backup line might have to pay only ¼ to ½ percent to have the line available, its borrowing cost should net out at least ½ percent below prime, and more usually 1 or 2 percent below prime. If you're dealing with borrowing needs of $100 million a year, the difference between selling commercial paper and borrowing from a bank at prime or above can be one or two million dollars, a substantial savings. If there is excess cash to lend to someone else, the financial executive charged with keeping loan costs down actually turns his or her department into a profit center.

Unfortunately, commercial paper isn't generally available to us as individuals. We can't sell it because we're not rated. I wanted you to get a basic idea of it so that you'll understand the executive who says he or she borrows money below prime all the time.

This short discussion of commercial paper may also give you some insight into an important dispute in banking, one which has already resulted in litigation. Remember our conversation about the prime rate, and the old definition of "the lowest rate available to the most creditworthy borrower." When the prime rate was in the teens and twenties during 1979–1982, quite a number of major Fortune 500 companies found that they could sell commercial paper at, say, 18 percent when the prime was at 21 percent. In such an environment, some of the banks, in order to keep their customers, had to lend to their most creditworthy customers at rates below prime. A Federal Reserve Board survey of forty-eight large banks showed that the percentage of below-prime loans rose from about 20 percent of all commercial loan extensions in the fourth quarter of 1978 to about 60 percent by the second quarter of 1980.[1]

That, of course, calls into question the very definition of the prime rate. The rest of us were still being quoted a "prime rate" which the banks were calling the rate it charged its most creditworthy customers. Yet some banks were charging their most creditworthy customers a lower rate. This *lower* rate, according to the definition, should have been the prime rate. Because major corporations threatened to sell commercial paper and because they have more dollar votes than you or I, they were able to negotiate better terms than prime.

There are now perhaps 50 lawsuits contending that

1. "Short-Term Business Lending at Rates Below the Prime Rate," an enclosure accompanying Exhibit E, a letter from Paul A. Volker, Chairman, Federal Reserve System, dated July 17, 1980, pages 318–327, FEDERAL MONETARY POLICY AND ITS EFFECT ON SMALL BUSINESS, PART 3. HEARINGS BEFORE A SUBCOMMITTEE ON ACCESS TO EQUITY CAPITAL AND BUSINESS OPPORTUNITIES OF THE HOUSE COMMITTEE ON SMALL BUSINESS., H. Rep., 96th Cong., 2nd Sess. (1980); See also, Quint, Michael, "Short-Term, Below Prime Rates to Big Customers Seem Permanent," *American Banker* (May 2, 1978).

banks should have lowered what they called their "prime rate" if they were making loans at those lower rates to their "most creditworthy customers." In *Kleiner* versus *First National Bank of Atlanta,*[2] Jackie Kleiner launched perhaps the first such lawsuit.

In the 1980 agreement for Mr. Kleiner's $415,000 real estate loan, First Atlanta charged 1 percent over prime, which was defined as the rate it charged its "best commercial borrowers" or its "best and most creditworthy borrowers." At the time, though, at least one of First Atlanta's most creditworthy borrowers was the Coca-Cola Company. Perhaps to entice Coca-Cola into borrowing from the bank, as opposed to selling commercial paper to raise money, First Atlanta was charging only 7¼ percent while announcing its "prime" to be 12¼ percent—and sending bills to Mr. Kleiner for 13¼ percent.[3]

When Kleiner sued, the bank's response was a heavy hand. According to Mr. Kleiner, a law professor for almost twenty years, the bank sought a criminal indictment against him for failing to disclose that he had once filed bankruptcy. This, the bank said, had not been disclosed and amounted to bank fraud. The charges were dropped by a grand jury when it was disclosed that the bank had indeed been aware of the bankruptcy and had, in fact, been a creditor in the proceedings.

This is what sent Mr. Kleiner to the law books where he discovered the civil use of the "Racketeering Influenced and Corrupt Organizations Act" or RICO for short. After he amended his lawsuit to include RICO claims (for treble damages and attorney's fees), the bank and its lawyers went a little crazy. Mr. Kleiner's lawsuit was a class action on behalf of all of First Atlanta's customers who were similarly situated. The bank's executives apparently asked its loan officers to call 4,000 of its borrowers and say, in effect, "we

2. See 526 F. Supp. 1019 (1981) (Note: "F.S." stands for Federal Supplement).
3. See *The New York Times,* February 3, 1984, page D1.

do not do business with our enemies." Of the total, 3,000 borrowers indicated an interest in "opting out" of the lawsuit.

But one of the bank's executives blew the whistle. Mr. Kleiner reports that this one man met with his minister, then with his family, went in one morning to resign and then showed up in the chambers of United States District Judge Orinda D. Evans to tell the story. In a 46 page opinion, Judge Evans disqualified the lawyers who were involved from further participation in the case, fined them $50,000, and ordered all of the customers reinstated as members of the class action. First Atlanta settled the case in March 1984 by agreeing to a $12.5 million settlement.[4]

I first learned of the *Kleiner* case in 1982 from a California bank executive who now believes that the old "most credit-worthy" definition is an open invitation to a lawsuit. Most, if not all, banks now define "prime" as being whatever rate they announce it to be.[5]

4. See *The Wall Street Journal,* March 22, 1984, page 28, col. 3.
5. See *An Analysis of Prime Rate Lending Practices at the Ten Largest United States Banks,* Staff Report, Comm. on Banking, Finance and Urban Affairs, H. Rep., 97th Cong., 1st Sess. (April 1981).

CHAPTER 17

Togetherness: Examples from the Orient

Now let's look at how we can obtain some of this power for ourselves, even if we aren't involved in businesses where demand deposits are inherently high.

In *Theory Z,* William G. Ouchi describes how the Japanese and Chinese have established social and financial networks respectively called "Tanomoshis" and "Huis." (Huis are relatively common in Hawaii, but there they are more like real estate investment syndicates than "revolving credit" societies.)

In a Tanomoshi or Hui each participant has a financial need. Someone wants to expand his business, another wants to buy new equipment, and so forth. There are usually about twelve people involved, but they aren't limited to participating in only one such group. Once each month, the members meet for dinner in the fashion of a dinner circuit. Each person brings $1,000 payable to the host and the host pays for dinner, but keeps $12,000. Over the course of a year, each person has paid for dinner, put in $12,000, and taken out $12,000. The advantage, of course, is that each host has a sum he or she might otherwise have difficulty saving at the time of the need.

Amazingly, there is no documentation and no collateral. The Japanese and Chinese are, to their credit, playing for the long-run return. No one would think of defaulting on an obligation to participate equally with the others because the long-run penalty—being excluded from the game (not to mention the personal disgrace)—is too severe. In the event that any one individual had difficulty meeting a monthly obligation, he or she would turn to another family member for support. Because the networking of the Tanomoshis and Huis is extensive, and because their philosophy is long term, the support is not hard to come by and is usually willingly given. Otherwise, all branches of the family might be banished from future participation.

In fact, not only is there no documentation or collateral, there is actually a *willingness* to be in someone's debt. In some societies, unlike ours, being in someone's debt is a sign of trust, not weakness. In these situations, it is considered rude to rush over and repay the debt. To do so would be taken as a sign that you were worried that your creditor would abuse the situation and ask you to perform some compensating obligation which would be difficult, distasteful, or burdensome.

For us, this kind of teamwork is relatively easy to understand intellectually, but very, very difficult to incorporate into our lives. Our social fabric is simply not woven with such memory, long-term thinking, and trust.

Theory Z describes how the Japanese have been able to achieve high levels of productivity because of high levels of trust, lifetime employment, and ten-year waits for promotions. In a *Theory Z* company, the employees are more productive because they care about the company's long-run success, not their own short-run promotions. Since each person is evaluated over a ten-year period and has the opportunity to work in a number of key positions, people do not compete with each other. They help their company compete with others. Anyone interested in self-aggrandizement will be asked to join an American firm.

Whether American firms can increase their productivity by remaking themselves into businesses with *Theory Z* characteristics is not the subject of this book. But we can take a cross-cut view of Ouchi's *Theory Z* and notice one of the hallmarks of Japanese industry—it's philosophy of banking. Each company, like the individual members of a Tanomoshi, is related to a large Japanese bank. They have circled their affairs around this bank like our own pioneers circled their wagons. When attacked (i.e., when a need arises), this circle, with the bank as a clearinghouse, is a wonderful resource. These clusters of firms, numbering from twenty to thirty, are called "Zaibatsus." In each cluster, there is a firm representing some major aspect of industrial society: a shipping firm, a steel maker, an insurance company, and so on. There is networking here. Clustered around each member firm of a Zaibatsu are a host of smaller, subordinate supplier companies. They cluster around the larger firms, the larger firms cluster around the banks, and the banks cluster around the omnipotent Ministry of International Trade and Industry (MITI).

The parallel between the organization of the Zaibatsu and the Tanomoshi is hard to miss. The upshot of this kind of interdependent networking is stability. With stability, however, comes a certain slowness in decision making. Decisions must be made and understood by consensus from top to bottom, which takes more time than we Americans generally will tolerate. In exchange for being slow, however, the *Theory Z* firm is able to *implement* change very quickly. Everyone knows what to do almost intuitively because they have heard about and participated in the decision. But above all, it is the long-term stability of a highly interdependent network which stands out as characteristic of the Zaibatsu and the Tanomoshi.

What would it take for us to develop such networks in the United States? Certainly it is self-defeating to impose it from on high. Our only hope, I think, is that such networks will come out of the one grouping we've always cherished: the family. It used to be that family members warned against borrowing from one another. If we were to set that warning aside in order to gain the financial power, vis a vis others, of the deposits we control together, then there might be sufficient incentive to make a start.

For example, I would readily bet that very few of us know much about the financial affairs of our grandparents, parents, brothers, or sisters. If this financial information were known, then it might be possible for the family to substantially improve its banking relationship at almost no additional expense.

For example, let's suppose that your father's business is prosperous and well established. It maintains checking account balances, in the ordinary course of business, of $50,-000. You need to buy a car, which these days might cost $15,000. You can afford $5,000 and need to finance the balance.

Fortunately, your father does not yet realize the value of his checking account. He keeps his business's money with Bank A, and his personal account at Bank B. And you bank with Bank C. Let's suppose, however, that your father bought his new car last year for cash (as he always does, having lived through the depression), and has no immediate need to use the power of his balances for himself. Let us also suppose that the two of you have a good relationship and can talk to each other. You do that and form a little "family partnership." Together, you approach the vice-president of Bank B, Charlie Banker. Prime is 10½ percent.

"Charlie," your father says, "I'm going to give you an opportunity to handle my business account, just like you've always wanted. But my son here wants to buy a car. We carry $50,000 in average collected balances in the business checking account and we want to borrow $10,000 for that new car he wants to buy. Those balances are worth something to you even if you pay us 5¼ percent for them and it's worth something to me to benefit my son. So we'd like to finance the new car with you for a lower-than-usual interest rate which will result in payments he can afford."

"Mr. Banker," you say, "I've calculated the yield that

the bank would have if you made this car loan to me at 4½ percent below prime (assuming prime is 11 percent), assuming certain other numbers (such as those in chapter 12, "Yield: the Sophisticated Approach"). The bank's return on asset yield is a whopping 9.97%. So instead of making a forty-eight-month car loan to me for $10,000 at 14 percent,

---

Borrower Name:	Loan Commitment: $

Loan Type:	New:	Renewal

Related Borrowers:	Officer:

Account Name:	Date:

Income

1. Requested Loan Amount	10,000	
2. Rate	6.5%	
3. Interest Earned on Requested Loan		$ 650
4. Average Balance of Existing Loans	N/A	
5. Average Rate		
6. Interest Earned on Existing Loan(s)		N/A
7. Average Total Loans	10,000	
8. Annualized Fees		N/A
9. Average Collected Balances	50,000	
DDA $50,000 Less 12% Reserve	44,000	
Time N/A Less 3% Reserve	N/A	
10. Net Balances	44,000	
11. Earnings Rate	8.8%	
(Prior 30 days average Fed funds rate)		
12. Earnings on Balances (Line 10 × 11)		3,872
13. Total Revenue		$4,522

Expenses

14. Cost of Funds: 9.0% × line 7	$ 900
(average of current 30 + 90 day C.D. Rates)	
15. Cost of Interest-Earning Deposits	
($50,000 × .0525)	2,625
16. Service and activity charges	N/A
17. Other Costs	N/A
18. Total Expenses	$3,525

Loan Profitability

19. Net Income (Line 13 − Line 18)	$997
20. Gross Yield % (Line 19 ÷ Line 7)	9.97%
21. Hurdle rate	5.0%
22. Over/(under)	4.97%

Fig. 17–1. Car Loan Hypothetical.

with payments of $273.30, you could well afford to make the loan to me at 6½ percent, so that my payments would be $237.13. Over the forty-eight months, that's $1,736.16 less than I might otherwise have to pay. But your yield is nevertheless a very big number. In fact, it's so big that I hope you understand when we ask for this kind of support again when my sister needs to replace her Datsun— with an American car."

"Well," replies Mr. Banker, "I don't think the loan committee will go for it. I admit I'd love to have your accounts, but we never loan money below prime. It's policy. But, how are you figuring?"

"I wrote it all out," you say. "Here." (See Fig. 17–1). If 4 percent covers cost of risk and overhead, the loan committee ought to love a net ROA yield of almost 5 percent.

"So Charles," says your dad, "you've always wondered what it would take to attract my business. I don't want more interest. You can attract others that way, but not me. I want a 4½ percent-below-prime car loan for my son. We can look at the balances every ninety days or so and see if I'm holding up my end of the bargain. If I am, that's the rate I want on this car loan. And you're gonna have a nice fat yield on the deposit/loan relationship. Why not run it by the committee? We're in no rush and I haven't even talked to my bank yet."

When (and if) Bank A hears that they stand to lose $50,000 in demand deposits, they will fight to keep them. They will have an equal or better deal approved through the president of the bank and the loan committee within a day or two. I've seen it happen.

CHAPTER 18

Increasing Your Balances

Once you've seen that cash in the form of demand deposits can make a difference, it makes sense to create more of it. In *Looking Out for Number 1*, Robert Ringer advises that you should constantly look for ways to keep someone else's dollar in your pocket for as long as possible. It's the basis for his "Financial-Geometric Growth Theory," otherwise known as "money makes money."

Ringer, a real estate broker, gives several examples of how to increase the amounts in your checking account starting with collecting security deposits. Since I share Ringer's real estate background, though not his dislike for Legalman, I've already discussed security deposits.

In addition to security deposits, Ringer cites the banks, utilities and finance companies for conceiving ways to get a hold of an extra few dollars from a lot of people, even for a little while. Utilities, Ringer says, do this by billing in advance and collecting for services they haven't yet provided. So they're a few days ahead of us.

American Express, he says, does even better. According to Ringer, American Express openly acknowledges a "float" in its traveler's checks business. They sell checks to us for cash and, from experience, they know those checks won't be used for an average of sixty-five days. So there's a two-month advantage.

The banks, Ringer contends, have perhaps the sweetest deal of all. As Ringer points out, we sometimes pay *them* a service charge to hold on to the money in our checking accounts for free. All year long. This is a "great laugher," Ringer chortles, for the banks.

Bill Mandel, a columnist for a San Francisco newspaper, recently discovered a version of this phenomenon, but he wasn't laughing. He stumbled onto his bank's practice of holding out-of-state checks submitted for deposit for ten to fifteen business days (fourteen or twenty-one calendar days) until the checks "clear." Only then was he allowed to draw against his money. Even though he made a "deposit," he didn't have the money. The money was either in the hands of the out-of-state bank (the payee bank) or his bank.

In Mr. Mandel's case, he deposited $10,000 on December 6, 1982. He was in the Mill Valley office of one of the largest national banks in the country. The payee bank was in New York City. The teller warned him to wait two weeks. He got a letter telling him to wait twenty-one days, until December 27, 1982, before writing any checks against this deposit. Meanwhile, he found out the New York City bank records showed the deduction from that account, for his check, on December 8.

This practice is a kind of reverse "float." Your money floats slowly *to* you. Mr. Mandel lost the use of his money for nineteen days and the bank used the deposits in the way I've described in this book and made a little extra interest income. Or, of course, it could have been a bureaucratic snafu. To discredit the latter hypothesis, however, Mr. Mandel cited two examples in his column. In his second case, someone else deposited a $10,000 check in a bank for a money-market account. The payee bank was in Boston. He was told to wait fifteen days for his money to begin working for him. In the meantime, the Boston bank's records showed the withdrawal and transfer to San Francisco only two days later.

The fast action is possible, of course, because computerization has made bank transfers, even cross-country transfers, far faster than it used to take for the mails. The "hold" for a short period of time to prevent check kiting (i.e., writing checks against bogus deposits) is, of course, legitimate. Asking us to wait for ten or fifteen days because we still think it takes that long to clear an out-of-state check is, on the other hand, taking advantage of our ignorance. (This volatile issue has already resulted in class-action litigation against banks.) The answer for you, if you've developed a better relationship with your banker because of his or her appreciation of your deposits, is to simply request a wire transfer. If that bank in New York wires the funds to that bank in California, it only takes a day. But you have to use magic words "wire transfer." See your banker to cut the red tape. If the deposit's large enough the fee is worth paying.

The point of these examples is that large corporations have been doing what I suggest that you do for a long time. They've become large and they stay large because they understand the power of *controlling* a large amount of money. While the large companies may invest the money they control and skim what they make over the time they have the principal, I suggest a variation on the theme for you. Hold onto someone else's dollar and increase the size of your demand deposits. Don't try to make money during the lag. Just use the power of the checking accounts you control to reduce your cost of borrowing. This improves your cash flow, your survivability, and your bottom line.

Let's make a checklist of some strategies that will increase your balances:

1. Get your income sooner;
2. Pay your bills later, but within a reasonable time;
3. Collect deposits and advances when you can;
4. Find a partner with accounts at a different bank, join up, and make a joint loan application based on the combined deposit levels;
5. Buy another company with more cash than you have.

You may recognize the opposite conditions or habits as old friends if:

1. You have a receivables problem;
2. You pay your bills immediately;
3. You shy away from retainers, deposits, advances, etc.;
4. You believe in the "rugged individualist" approach, to the extent that you always go it alone and won't form networks or partnerships with family or friends.

Some of what I've said may sound aggressive. Pay your bills later? That hardly seems gentlemanly. But that's not the point. Robert Ringer may have sounded crass when he wrote *Looking Out for #1* (remember that he's a broker), but most of us admitted he was being realistic. The point is to take action in your own interest (excuse the pun). For every effort you make at reasonably delaying writing a check against your precious balances, there is someone on the receiving end trying to get your check before the ink is dry. But there are methods available to help forestall those payments. No matter where you live in the country, there are companies that can tell you how long it takes mail to get from one post office to another. If you sell nationally, checks are coming to you from all over. And although your corporate office may be in New York, you'll actually get your money a day or two faster if you have your customers send it to Pittsburgh, St. Louis, or Dallas, for example, where the postal turnaround times are the quickest. For the largest companies, even hours can make a substantial difference. On the other hand, the studies can also tell you from where you should mail your checks, i.e., from the cities which are found to have the slowest service. If you mail from New York City, Chicago, or Atlanta, your check will get there later, not sooner, and your balances will stay higher longer.

I suggest delays, however, only to a point. If you're delinquent to the point of hurting your credit rating, you're throwing the baby out with the bathwater. Ideally, you should pay your bills the day before your creditor's internal receivables management system notices that you're late.

There is always some lag in this system because of the expense of holding short reins on everyone at the same time.

In short, if your business doesn't inherently involve large checking account balances, do what you can to increase the balances you have or control. Think about your business and see if there aren't one or two ways to increase your balances without being so obvious about your intentions that your clients or creditors take offense.

One approach to controlling someone else's deposits is to make them the reward in a contest. Let's make a proposal to a hypothetical employer to create a new fringe benefit. Your company undoubtedly has more money and a stronger banking relationship than you do. Since it *is* possible for a banker to allocate a portion of your company's balances to any other account, it's possible to strengthen your balances by borrowing some of the company's. This takes personal attention by the banker, but this assignment of profitability from one account to another is feasible. It can't be done, of course, without your company's consent. That shouldn't be hard to get, however, once you explain that you are only talking about assigning a small portion of the average balances *to the most productive employee of the year.*

The great virtue of this is that it's a wonderful way for the company to tap into promoting increased productivity among employees and a wonderful way for employees to tap into the power of their company's balances and banking relationship—all with very little, if any, expense to the company because the company will probably be using a resource that hasn't been exploited before or which may be diluted to an infinitesimal degree.

As individuals, we could also take the novel approach of cooperating with each other. Formally, this is usually done by forming a partnership. A partnership could be a complex agreement. Let me simplify things a bit. For my example, we'll discuss promissory notes. A partnership would be composed of a series of these notes and each partner, at different times, would be a borrower and lender. The whole point would be to magnify each person's individual financial power for a certain period of time and then to reciprocate.

The natural place for this to first occur is among family. But with family members we have to be careful and draw up notes, lest the IRS treat the transaction as a gift. Using a note also protects the lender in case something goes wrong. Without a note, a lender could be in serious trouble: in addition to having the loan appear as a gift, the lender might not be able to claim a bad-debt deduction.

Also, because gifts of only $10,000 per person per year are exempt from a gift tax, a transaction without a note could result in a tax on the lender.

A note is a simple thing, really. In effect, it acknowledges receipt for the money and expresses the terms under which it will be repaid.

Here's a sample promissory note for a family loan.

Promissory Note (Unsecured)

In exchange for value received, the undersigned promises to pay to _____ (beneficiary), at _____,
                                Name   Address
the sum of $_____ with interest at the rate of
                    Amount
_____% per annum, as follows: [interest only in equal monthly installments on the first day of each month; principal all due and payable on _____] OR [$_____ per month on the first day of each month; unpaid principal and all unpaid interest, if any, due and payable on _____].

In the event of a default, the beneficiary may declare the entire amount of unpaid principal and interest immediately due and payable. [Note: This is an "acceleration clause" and is optional].

Payment shall be in lawful money of the United States. In the event of a dispute, the prevailing party is entitled to recover costs, disbursements, and reasonable attorney's fees for any negotiation or pretrial, trial, or postjudgment proceeding including any appeal.

Dated: _____   _____
                                          Maker

For an interest-free loan, the note should be changed to read that it is payable "on demand."

In order to make the note saleable to someone else, it should read that it is payable to the lender (i.e., beneficiary), or "order." The beneficiary can then endorse the note and assign it to someone else in exchange for payment, often at a discount.

For our purposes, a family loan, the promissory note included in the text is *not* a negotiable instrument. There is no "or order" phrase and the matter is strictly between borrower and lender. This tends to keep the matter *within* the family.

We can also use a family loan to accomplish a number of goals. While our first goal is to beef up the borrower's cash position before dealing with a bank (the real lender), we can also use it to shift income from higher- to lower-bracket taxpayers.

For example, let's take three $10,000 loans from parents, grandparents, and godparents (our lenders) to the young married couple needing two $11,250 cars in order to work at their respective jobs. They have the monthly income to make the payments, but they are faced with having to pay high rates on a loan amortized over three or four years.

We'll assume that the lenders can't afford to tie up their money for too long and that the parents have a substantial income but that the grandparents and godparents are retired.

To solve our problem, we write three promissory notes. The loan from the parents bears no interest because they already have a substantial income. They don't need the extra interest income. The loans from the grandparents and godparents is for 20 percent,[1] to supplement their social security retirement checks. Since their level of income is presumably much lower, this income is only slightly taxed. When the car loans are repaid, the deposits can be freed, and the interest

---

1. The 20 percent figure raises the issue of usury. Usury is a rate which exceeds the maximum lawful rate. This varies from state to state.

can be forgiven or counted towards principal, as the parties choose.

But now we have $30,000 to offer the bank when we go looking for $22,500 in loans. Let's continue with all of the other assumptions I've used before, namely that prime is at 11 percent, and so on. With $30,000 in deposits, our young

Borrower Name:	Loan Commitment: $	
Loan Type:	New:	Renewal
Related Borrowers:	Officer:	
Account Name:	Date:	

Income

1. Requested Loan Amount	22,500	
2. Rate	5.5%	
3. Interest Earned on Requested Loan		$1,237.50
4. Average Balance of Existing Loans	N/A	
5. Average Rate	N/A	
6. Interest Earned on Existing Loan(s)		N/A
7. Average Total Loans	22,500	
8. Annualized Fees		N/A
9. Average Collected Balances	30,000	
DDA $30,000 Less 12% Reserve	26,400	
Time N/A Less 3% Reserve	N/A	
10. Net Balances	26,400	
11. Earnings Rate	8.8%	
(Prior 30 days average Fed funds rate)		
12. Earnings on Balances (Line 10 × 11)		2,323.20
13. Total Revenue		$3,560.70

Expenses

14. Cost of Funds: 9.0% × line 7	$2,025
(average of current 30 + 90 day C.D. Rates)	
15. Cost of Interest-Earning Deposits	
(calculate separately)	N/A
16. Service and activity charges	N/A
17. Other Costs	N/A
18. Total Expenses	$2,025

Loan Profitability

19. Net Income (Line 13 − Line 18)	$1,423.20
20. Gross Yield % (Line 19 ÷ Line 7)	6.3%
21. Hurdle Rate	5.0%
22. Over/(under)	1.3%

Fig. 18–1. Pooled Resources Example.

borrowers can negotiate rates for their cars at 5½ percent below prime, or 5½ percent, and become valued customers of their bank (see Fig. 18–1). They'll have their cars and their careers, and all without a financial anchor to slow them down. Since our young borrowers are working and have a substantial income, their cash flow won't be constricted and they can concentrate on advancing their careers and earning even more. And, in the bargain, we've shifted income from high-bracket to low-bracket taxpayers.

Let's continue our scenario but advance it by four years. The car loans have been repaid and the three $10,000 loans are due. Of course, it's easy to repay them because the money's always been on hand in our borrowers' checking accounts.

Every once in a while you'll notice that the banks get together as a consortium in order to make a really large loan. This is called a "participation." In such a syndicate of lenders, there is usually a lead bank which has recognized that the loan is too large (that is, the risk is too great in case of loss) for an institution of its size to handle alone. So it asks

other banks to take a piece of the action and become partici-
pants. In really large lending projects, there might be ten or
twenty participating banks.

Now that we've reviewed the reason why the big boys
get together—to spread the risk—we can see a good reason
to create a *borrowing* syndicate—to lower the cost of borrowing.

Our purpose, of course, is different. We're not spreading
the risk, we're increasing our power, our clout.

I've already talked about the concept of such a syndicate when I noted that family members could help each
other simply by keeping all of their various accounts at the
same bank. The mere threat of moving all of the accounts at
once should encourage your banker to grant you services,
favors, and low-interest loans.

The idea behind the teamwork of a borrower's confederation is to magnify the power and importance of any one
person's resources.

Forming such a team of players in this game is probably
easier said than done. My suggestion is to begin with already
formed groups such as bridge clubs, poker partners, sewing
circles, and investment clubs.

Before this audience with a potential banker, of course,
the "partners" need to meet and agree among themselves.
An agreement which could form the basis for discussion, and
which could be tailored to meet the special goals or consider-
ations of any group, is set forth at the end of this chapter.
Please note, before using it, that a borrower's syndicate, confederation, or cartel (whatever you call it) is an innovative
and new idea. Anyone forming such a group must proceed at
his or her own risk and with counsel (so you aren't accused of
practing law without a license). My goal is to provide you
with a starting point, but that's all I can do.

PARTNERSHIP AGREEMENT

This Agreement is made on _____, by and between _____, _____, referred to as "Partners"
under the following provisions.

1. The Partners shall associate to form a General Partnership for the purpose of borrowing money, and any other business agreed upon by the Partners.

2. The Partnership name shall be "Borrowers Confederation of America."

3. The Partnership shall commence on _____ and shall continue until dissolved by agreement of the Partners or terminated under the provisions of this Agreement.

4. The Partnership's principal place of business shall be at _____. The Partnership shall maintain any other place or places of business agreed upon by the Partners.

5. The Partnership's initial capital shall be Fifty Thousand Dollars ($50,000.00). Each Partner shall contribute toward the initial capital by depositing the following amounts in the Partnership checking or savings acccount at the _____ ("Bank"), or any other bank selected by a majority of the Partners, on or before _____.

_____ shall contribute Ten Thousand Dollars ($10,000.00) (referred to as Partner 1);

_____ shall contribute Ten Thousand Dollars ($10,000.00) (referred to as Partner 2);

_____ shall contribute Ten Thousand Dollars ($10,000.00) (referred to as Partner 3);

_____ shall contribute Ten Thousand Dollars ($10,000.00) (referred to as Partner 4);

_____ shall contribute Ten Thousand Dollars ($10,000.00) (referred to as Partner 5);

The order and priority accorded to each such Partner in this Paragraph 5 shall be determined by draw.

6. No Partner shall withdraw any portion of the Partnership capital without the other Partner's express written consent.

7. The Partners intend that each of them will borrow up to Forty-Five Thousand Dollars ($45,000) from the Bank with which the Partnership has its checking or savings account on a rotating basis (i.e., first Partner 1, then Partner 2, . . . , etc.) each for a period of six (6) months. Each such Partner shall negotiate the terms of said Bank loan to his or her best advantage given their individual financial statement and the Partnership funds on deposit at the Bank. Each such Partner shall make a good-faith effort to negotiate his or her

loan from the Bank by maintaining the Partnership funds in the highest interest-bearing account consistent with that Partner's efforts to reduce the cost of the loan from the Bank. Any Partner may pass his or her turn in rotation, in which case the next Partner in order shall have the benefit of the Partnership accounts.

8. The Partners shall share equally in any Partnership net profits and shall bear Partnership losses equally.

9. Partnership books of account shall be accurately kept and shall include records of all Partnership income, expenses, assets, and liabilities. The Partnership books of account shall be maintained on a semiannual basis. Each Partner shall have the right to inspect the Partnership books at any time.

10. The Partnership's fiscal year shall end on December 31 of each year.

11. Complete accountings of the Partnership affairs at the close of business on the last days of June and December of each year shall be rendered to each Partner within sixty (60) days after the close of each such month. At the time of each accounting, the net profits of the Partnership shall be distributed to the Partners as provided in this Agreement. Except as to errors brought to the Partners' attention within thirty (30) days after it is rendered, each accounting shall be final and conclusive.

12. Each Partner shall be obligated to devote only so much time to the Partnership business as is reasonable. Nothing herein shall prevent any Partner from engaging in any other business or occupation whether or not it involves any other Partner.

13. Each Partner shall have an equal right in the management of the Partnership. Each Partner shall have authority to bind the Partnership in making contracts and incurring obligations in the Partnership name or on its credit. No Partner, however, shall incur obligations in the Partnership name or on its credit exceeding One Thousand Dollars ($1,000.00) without the other Partners' express written consent. Any obligation incurred in violation of this provision shall be charged to and collected from the Partner who incurred the obligation.

14. No Partner shall be entitled to any compensation for services to the Partnership. The Partners may, however,

declare a bonus to one or more Partners at any time by mutual agreement of the Partners.

15. The term "net profits," as used in this Agreement, shall mean the Partnership net profits as determined by generally accepted accounting principles for each accounting period specified in this Agreement.

16. After ninety (90) days written notice of intent to the Partners, any Partner may withdraw from the Partnership at the end of any accounting period specified in this Agreement. At the time of withdrawal, the withdrawing Partner shall be entitled to receive a return of his or her remaining capital. The Partners may replace a withdrawing Partner by admitting a new Partner. In the event of a withdrawal, the Partner next in order shall take the place of the withdrawing Partner and every other Partner shall advance their number by one. The newly admitted Partner shall be assigned the lowest available number. No withdrawing Partner may ever rejoin the Partnership.

16. On the death, withdrawal, or other act of either Partner, the remaining Partners may continue the Partnership by purchasing the outgoing Partner's interest in the Partnership. The remaining Partners shall purchase the outgoing Partner's interest by paying to the outgoing Partner or the appropriate personal representative the outgoing Partner's capital account plus any "interest" as determined under Paragraph 17 of this Agreement.

17. A Partner's "interest" shall mean the outgoing Partner's undisbursed net profits as determined by the last regular accounting preceding dissolution plus the full unwithdrawn portion of the outgoing Partner's share in net profits earned between the date of such accounting and the date of dissolution.

18. In the event of death of any Partner, the remaining Partners shall have ninety (90) days from the date of death in which to purchase the deceased Partner's partnership interest. The purchase price shall be the Partner's capital account plus the deceased Partner's interest as determined under Paragraph 17 of this Agreement. During the ninety (90) day period following a Partner's death, the remaining Partners may continue the Partnership business. The liability of the deceased Partner's estate for Partnership obligations incurred

during the period of continuation shall be limited to the remaining capital of the deceased Partner at the time of death.

19. On any purchase and sale made pursuant to Paragraphs 16, 17, or 18 of this Agreement, the remaining Partners shall assume all Partnership obligations. The remaining Partners shall hold the withdrawing Partner or the deceased Partner's estate and personal representative, free and harmless from all liability for Partnership obligations. Immediately upon purchase of a withdrawing or deceased Partner's interest, the remaining Partners shall prepare, file, serve, and publish all notices required by law to protect the withdrawing Partner or the deceased Partner's estate and personal representative from liability for future Partnership obligations. All costs incident to the requirements of this Paragraph shall be borne by the withdrawing Partner or the estate of a deceased Partner.

20. On dissolution of the Partnership, except as provided in Paragraphs 16, 17, and 18 of this Agreement, the Partnership affairs shall be wound up, the Partnership assets liquidated, its debts paid, and the surplus divided among the Partners according to their remaining capital accounts in the Partnership business.

21. All notices between the Partners shall be in writing and shall be deemed served when personally delivered to a Partner, or when deposited in the United States mail, certified, first-class postage prepaid, addressed to a Partner at his or her residence address or to such other place as may be specified in a notice given pursuant to this Paragraph as the address for service of notice on such Partner.

22. All consents and agreements provided for or permitted by this Agreement shall be in writing. Signed copies of all consents and agreements pertaining to the Partnership shall be kept with the Partnership books.

23. On all accountings provided for in this Agreement, the goodwill of the Partnership business shall be valued at one dollar ($1) and no more.

24. This instrument contains the Partner's sole agreement relating to their Partnership. It correctly sets out the Partners' rights and obligations. Any prior agreements, promises, negotiations, or representations not expressly set forth in this instrument have no meaning.

25. In the event of any dispute between the Partnership and any Partner or between a Partner and any other Partner concerning rights or duties hereunder, the prevailing parts shall be entitled to recover all costs, disbursements, and reasonable attorney's fees from the other party, including any postjudgment proceeding and any appeal.

Executed _____ at _____ County, _____ on _____.

_____
Partner 1

_____
Partner 2

_____
Partner 3

_____
Partner 4

_____
Partner 5

CHAPTER 19

Pitfalls

As you may recall, my original deal did *not* involve tying up or freezing my demand deposits. If a banker wants to impose this kind of restriction on you, it would obviously be a pitfall, primarily because such a demand betokens a lack of trust. If your banker wants to freeze your deposits, it's either because the deal is too thin and perhaps shouldn't be made in the first place or because he or she doubts that you'll maintain your balances after the deal has been struck.

From a practical point of view, you can't allow such a freeze. If your banker somehow fails to live up to the bargain, you need the freedom to move your balances. From a legal standpoint, however, a freeze may be a bad deal for the banker. This is because a freeze on your deposits (meaning that you can no longer control them) might amount to an offset on the effective amount of money the bank is lending to you. Even if the interest rate on the *loan* is less than the maximum allowed by law, the principal is in effect reduced by the "freeze offset," which could result in a usurious rate. Since your banker certainly will not want the transaction challenged as being usurious, you ought to be able to succeed in your argument that your deposits should not be frozen.

In this regard, you might refer your banker to *American Timber & Trading Co.* versus *First National Bank of Oregon*, decided on October 22, 1982 by the Ninth Circuit Court of Appeals.[1] This was a class action suit against a national bank, in which a group of depositors claimed that loans for which the bank charged a legal rate of interest (the maximum legal rate was 10 percent per annum) were in fact usurious because the bank required that demand deposits equal to 10 percent of the loan be kept on hand at the bank. The demand deposits were non-interest bearing and *frozen*. The argument, which was successful on appeal, was based on simple mathematics. Let's suppose that the bank was lending $100,000 at 9.5 percent. During a year, the resulting interest income would be $9,500. But suppose the bank required a non-interest-bearing deposit of $10,000 at the time the loan was made and suppose further that the borrower would be unable to withdraw these funds during the term of the loan. Under these circumstances, the bank is effectively lending only $90,000 and the effective rate of interest is increased. The effective interest is found by dividing the interest income—$9,500—by the new principal—$90,000, with the result being 10.55 percent. If the maximum rate allowed by law is 10 percent, the transaction is usurious, even though the stated rate of interest is only 9.5 percent.

For many banks, a usurious transaction results in horrible public relations. And, in addition, such a transaction can be very expensive. In some states, a borrower who has actually paid usurious interest is entitled to treble damages— three times the amount of excess interest actually paid. For a nationally chartered bank, the damages are figured differently. Although the multiplier here is only two instead of three, it is taken against all of the interest actually paid, not

1. 690 F.2d 781 (9th Cir. 1982) (Note: "F.2d" stands for Federal Reporter, Second Series.)

just that portion which exceeds the legal maximum. In *American Timber & Trading Co. v. First National Bank of Oregon,* for example, one class of borrowers paid $3,372 in excess interest. Trebled, this amount would have been only $10,116. However, since the total amount of interest was doubled, the award was for $422,295.68!

On the other hand, and this is just as we would want it, there is at least one case holding that there is no usury where the compensating balance amounts remained the property of the *borrower* even though they were eventually applied to repayment of the loan. This is a Louisiana case known as *Deposit Guaranty National Bank* versus *Shipp,*[2] decided in 1968.

However, you may meet a banker who says that he or she would love to have your balances and that they are indeed worth something, but that the bank has to save face by writing its loan for a standard rate. The proposal is to pay the borrower a fee or unusually high interest on the balances (instead of dropping the rate on the loan). What this amounts to is paying interest on a checking account. Under what was known as Regulation Q, this used to be illegal and something that bank examiners looked for. It was a risk for everyone. Usually an aggressive banker would agree to pay a certain percentage on the balances, and then the borrower and banker would contrive some consulting agreement or the like as the vehicle for paying the borrower. The payment under such a contract was a payment for bringing in and maintaining certain balances, whether there was a loan outstanding or not. The "consulting" services to be rendered were ephemeral and easy for the depositor to fulfill with practically no work at all.

This is not the problem it used to be. Regulation Q is being phased out and banks are all scrambling to the marketplace, along with every other kind of financial institution,

2. 205 So. 101, 105 (La. App. 1968); Other cases are collected in Annot., Leaving Part of Loan on Deposit with Lender as Usury, 92 A.L.R. 3d 769 (1979) (Note: "So." stands for the Southern Reporter; "A.L.R. 3d" stands for American Law Reports, Third Series.)

with varying schemes that pay interest on checking account balances. These are the accounts with the catchy names, names such as "Ultimate Checking," the "Cash Maximizer Account," and The "Market Rate Account." You open accounts like these with $1,000 and there is no service charge if you maintain balances of at least $2,500.

The reason the banks can now offer interest on certain checking accounts is because Congress passed the Depository Institutions Deregulation and Monetary Control Act of 1980 (Omnibus Banking Act)[3] and the Garn-St. Germain Depository Institutions Act of 1982. The Garn-St. Germain Act made it legal for banks to offer interest on checking accounts of at least $2,500.[4]

The 1980 Omnibus Banking Act eliminates, among other things, the rules limiting the rates of interest which federally insured savings and loan associations, banks, and other institutions may pay on deposits. This is the six-year phaseout of Regulation Q. With the Omnibus Banking Act, the savings and loans also won the right to allow depositors to write checks against their savings accounts. These are the Negotiable Order of Withdrawal or "NOW" accounts. Many of the savings and loans are delighted to look like

---

3. The Act provides for the eventual elimination of interest rate ceilings. For example, the ¼ percent differential formerly enjoyed by savings and loans over banks was eliminated on October 1, 1983.
4. Garn-St. Germain accelerated the deregulation process. Under it, mergers and reorganizations are facilitated, primarily to benefit the companies in danger of going under. More importantly, certain restrictions on all lending activities by national banks were removed, the investment powers of thrift institutions were expanded, and the depository abilities of all banking institutions were liberalized.

Because of yet another aspect of Garn-St. Germain, known as the "Thrift Institutions Restructurizing Act" (Title III of Garn-St. Germain), federal savings and loans were authorized to accept demand deposits from commercial corporate and agricultural customers with a loan relationship. Finally the savings and loans could offer checking accounts, just like banks. The state savings and loans, arguing a need for parity with the federal savings and loan down the street, quickly won the same right.

banks by being able to offer checking accounts and other similar services. In fact, many of them like to market themselves as banks. For example, First Federal Savings & Loan changed its name to First Federal Savings Bank of California. And Allstate Savings changed its name to Sears Savings Bank.

What we're seeing is homogenization as a byproduct of deregulation. There's a double benefit in this new trend for us customers. First, more financial institutions will be competing with each other. Institutions we call banks will be competing both with other banks *and* with institutions we now call savings and loans. Second, with deregulation, these financial institutions will be unable to hide behind a law that makes them safe from having to really deal with their customers. It used to be that a banker could say, "Look, we pay the legal maximum rate of 5¼ percent on our savings accounts and you can't get a better deal from anyone else." Well, with deregulation, banking will become more competitive. The impossible deal of yesterday may be feasible today if you're persistent and knowledgeable.

Many financial institutions started advertising these new accounts during the fall of 1982 with full-page newspaper ads and commercials on TV and radio. Their thirst for demand and interest-bearing accounts underscores what I've been saying in this book. Nothing in our economic structure really has changed. What banks were willing to do surreptitiously when Regulation Q was in effect, they are willing to do publicly now that Regulation Q is being phased out and interest-rate competition is in. Banks and savings and loans are now heavily advertising the fact that they're willing to pay you for your accounts.

One effect of the competition, the higher rates, and the advertising is that the mix between checking accounts and interest-bearing savings (time) accounts is changing. Before the Garn-St. Germain Act took effect in December 1982, about 35 percent of a bank's accounts were checking accounts; the other 65 percent were savings accounts. Since passage of the Act, the mix has changed, at least according to one bank president. About 30 percent of the accounts are checking accounts; the other 70 percent are savings accounts. Bankers view this change as an increase in their cost of funds. They have to pay interest on more of the money they hold. I view it as an opportunity because my non-interest-bearing checking account is all the more rare and desirable.

What bankers haven't said, and won't say, is *why* the checking account balances are valuable to them and how much that value really amounts to. Actually, you can't blame them. They're offering as little as they can get away with offering. So long as the marketplace is beset with imperfect information (and it always is), they will continue to do so. When we start demanding more and negotiating from the position of strength which we really have (because *we* have the money), their offers will go up and our costs will go down.

CHAPTER 20

The Leveraged Buy-Out

Suppose we form a family partnership and take on a larger project. Instead of buying a car, let's buy another company. While this is something of a tangent, it will illustrate the approach I've been outlining in a scaled-up business context.

Although the example I'll work with is completely fictional, it's composed of elements out of my own experience. Let's suppose initially that we own and operate a farm whose crops are apples and pears. Our business is good, but we are only farmers. Once our produce is picked, our work is done and our worry begins. That's because our crop is trucked to the central market and sold for the best price by commission merchants who receive the apples and pears from us and many other growers. They sell to the chain-store grocers for a commission. We get the best price our commission merchant is able to negotiate, less freight and their commission. Because of this business structure, we're interested in a vertical integration; i.e., acquiring another company in a direct line from farmer to consumer.

Our position is analogous to that of a manufacturer interested in acquiring a distributor. As farmers, we're interested in acquiring our wholesaler because it's this step in our own particular business that determines our sales price (unless, of course, we sell to the merchant and let him have the difference between his price to us and the price he gets from the markets).

So, let's think about our target. Our potential acquisition is different from buying a car because a going business has a multitude of assets. One of them is cash. We learn that commission merchants need a substantial amount of ready cash because they face weekly payrolls, because they want to take advantage of purchase opportunities, and because we farmers present a constant demand for payment on the produce previously consigned. You have to handle a large volume to make any money because the profit margin is a razor-thin 2 or 3 percent. But if you have volume, the rewards are substantial because the volume is substantial. It's a good business if you don't mind getting up for a day that starts at midnight.

Now let's assume that we've found a willing seller and actually settled on a price for the assets of the business. We'll pay $250,000 for the inventory, trucks, warehouse, and miscellaneous office equipment. This is different from buying stock. With stock, you get the assets and the liabilities. But here we only want assets, even if the price may be higher, because we want to negotiate our own debt structure. Since we're willing to pay cash, we've been able to obtain a good price. So far, so good.

Our chief problem, of course, is that we don't have the cash. Instead of $250,000, we only have $100,000 (the equity side of our financing) and we need to borrow the balance (our debt financing). Fortunately, we bank with someone who understands a deposit/loan relationship.

But suppose our own deposit relationship is not strong enough to support a favorable pricing decision on a $150,000 loan. This is often the case. *So we look to the assets we're going to acquire.* If our target already banks with the same bank we do, our banker will already be familiar with the account. There is something even more promising about being able to move a new account to our bank. For us, it's part of our negotiating strength with our banker. For our banker, it's a feather in his or her cap to have gained this new and substantial account.

Let's look at our target again. While the cash we acquire at the close of escrow may not be substantial, we care, and our banker cares, about the average collected balances the business seems to generate month in and month out. These are numbers you would be able to determine during the financial investigation you would undertake prior to closing. You would want to see the company's bank statements and they would generally be disclosed to you. You would want to see them as backup for the income statements which show revenue and expenses for any given period. In our hypothetical example, let's suppose that our commission merchant has annual revenues of about two million dollars and average ledger balances of $75,000.

So, we want to borrow $150,000 and we can offer our target's $75,000 in balances in order to negotiate for favorable terms on the acquisition loan. Notice that we are now borrowing twice the amount of our average balances. In previous examples, balances exceeded loans.

Without being particularly precise, let's suppose that we can show a reasonable likelihood that our operation of the business would generate sufficient revenue to not only cover operating expenses but the cost of our debt financing. If our bank has confidence in our ability to run the business and our enhanced ability to repay this new debt (because of the new revenue and profit), then the underwriting decision can be made in favor of the loan.

Now the issue is pricing, and that's where the average collected balances come in. If we had ignored the power of our target's balances, we would have had to pay a market rate for the loan (i.e., prime plus 2 or 3), or miss the opportunity altogether. In addition, we might have had to pay a loan-origination fee in the form of points and, no doubt, we would have been faced with more demanding repayment terms. With less favorable terms, the interest expense and cash flow burdens might have been too great.

Without utilizing the advantage of the assets we planned on acquiring in a creative way, the transaction might not have been possible. Using the hurdle pricer, and assuming the same rates as in our other examples, we see that the terms might be ¾ percent below prime, with no points (see Figure 20–1).

This, in essence, is a leveraged buy-out. We look to the

Borrower Name:	Loan Commitment:	$
Loan Type:	New:	Renewal
Related Borrowers:	Officer:	
Account Name:	Date:	

Income

1. Requested Loan Amount	150,000	
2. Rate	10.25%	
3. Interest Earned on Requested Loan		$15,375
4. Average Balance of Existing Loans	N/A	
5. Average Rate	N/A	
6. Interest Earned on Existing Loan(s)		N/A
7. Average Total Loans	150,000	
8. Annualized Fees		N/A
9. Average Collected Balances	75,000	
DDA $75,000 Less 12% Reserve	66,000	
Time ___ Less 3% Reserve	N/A	
10. Net Balances	66,000	
11. Earnings Rate	8.8%	
(Prior 30 days average Fed funds rate)		
12. Earnings on Balances (Line 10 × 11)		5,808
13. Total Revenue		$21,183

Expenses

14. Cost of Funds: 9.0% × line 7		$13,500
(average of current 30 + 90 day C.D. Rates)		
15. Cost of Interest-Earning Deposits		
(calculate separately)		N/A
16. Service and Activity Charges		N/A
17. Other Costs		N/A
18. Total Expenses		$13,500

Loan Profitability

19. Net Income (Line 13 − Line 18)		$7,683
20. Gross Yield % (Line 19 ÷ Line 7)		5.1%
21. Hurdle Rate		5.0%
22. Over/(under)		.1%

Fig. 20–1. Leveraged Buy-Out Hypothetical.

assets of the company we plan to acquire and negotiate for better loan terms on the strength of assets not yet ours. When this kind of transaction works, it's beautiful. What allows it to work is the use of someone else's assets (in this case the checking account of the company you want to buy) in a way the present owners have never used them. This creativity makes the deal interesting and feasible at the same time. Multiply the numbers I've used by 10, 100, or 1,000, and you'll understand the thinking behind the leveraged buy-outs of Fortune 500 companies.

As a final thought on the subject of buy-outs, you might be interested to know of a new section to the Internal Revenue Code. Although it has a limited purpose, banks are responding to it with offers of loans below prime. Section 133 of the Code was added on July 18, 1984, and applies to loans made after that date. It states that banks and certain other lenders need not include 50 percent of their gross interest income received on loans to an employer corporation or an employee stock ownership plan (known as an ESOP) when the money is used to acquire employer securities. With this tax break, a below-prime loan is easy to justify even without any depositor relationship. Some banks have offered ESOP loans at 80 percent of prime. With a deposit relationship as well, based on the principles explained in this book, you ought to be able to drive the rates significantly below prime. With this kind of financing, groups of employees may become far more significant owners of Corporate America than ever before.

CHAPTER 21

Raising Our Sights
to See the Forest

We've made one transition so far, scaling up our thinking from an auto loan to an acquisition of a going business. The only reason we've been able to do this is because the concepts of money, borrowing, interest rates, and so on are common to each one.

But all of our individual transactions take place in an even larger context. We have dollar votes to cast in a very large popularity contest known as the money market.

The largest player in this national marketplace is the federal government. The National Association of Manufacturers estimated that, as recently as 1979, the federal government was taking only 19 percent of the money raised by borrowing. In 1984 the National Association of Manufacturers estimates that our record yearly deficits could force Washington into gobbling up as much as *60 percent* of the money available for borrowing. This is such a large demand on our national money supply that all of us are affected by it. It's very hard to compete with such a large borrower who, unlike the rest of us, has no limit on what it will spend to obtain the market share it needs.

So, while you and I might try our best to be clever and resourceful, we're still talking about how to beat the conditions imposed on us by still larger forces. At any given time, we're faced with a market prime rate and we have to negotiate around it. The forces that keep these rates high in general are forces that should concern us as well. After all, we are all shareholders in Uncle Sam, at least philosophically. If Uncle Sam has trouble and rates are high, the pressure on us will increase significantly even if we can beat the game and borrow at rates below prime.

Most of what we've discussed so far will only apply in a general way to these following last chapters. In them, I'm going to describe the scary financial situation as shown by documents published by our very own government. In this particular endeavor, I am acting only as a reporter and commentator.

Now, let's go on to the level of viewing our country as one large national business enterprise. We will leave the idea of borrowing money below prime behind, and look at the general conditions which made the rates so high in the first place.

CHAPTER 22

The Financial Condition
of the United States

Very few people are aware of the existence of a detailed set of consolidated financial statements which are prepared annually by the Controller General. I obtained my copy with a simple letter shown in Figure 22–1. It is also available at major libraries. I only learned of their existence during 1982, and sometimes I wonder if I wasn't better off not knowing. Well, it's too late for me to turn back the clock and now it's too late for you too. While this chapter may seem to digress from the topic of borrowing below prime, you will soon see its broader relevance. What made it so urgent to find a way to borrow below prime were the conditions that led to a high prime rate in the first place. In this chapter, we'll begin to use our new awareness of money and its cost to understand the forces which *generate* a high prime rate.

It's not my intention that you gain a total understanding of the consolidated financial statements of the United States. Frankly I don't believe that there is anyone in the world that can honestly say he (or she) understands them.

July 28, 1983

Department of the Treasury
Bureau of Government Financial Operations
Division of Government
Accounts and Reports
Washington, D.C.   20226

     Ref: *G-GR-SRB-MOB*

Gentlemen:

     Please forward a copy of the "Consolidated Financial Statements of the United States" to me at your earliest convenience. Please let me know if there is any cost.

Very truly yours,

Nelson E. Brestoff

Fig. 22-1. Sample Letter to Obtain U.S. Financial Statements.

This is not meant as a criticism. It's the result of the incredible magnitude and complexities of that nonprofit business known as the United States of America.

     My hope is to give you some insight into certain general and specific components of the financial picture of the country. You may not like what you read and you may not believe it, but I think it will start you thinking and asking questions.

     In June, 1982, the most current financial statement available was for the fiscal year ending September 30, 1981. With one exception I will use the September 30, 1981 figures as a basis for this chapter. Although the "notes" are said to be an integral part of the statement, I have not included them, in part because the statements are unaudited, but primarily because the point is to see the forest, not the trees.

     Before I get into the specific facts regarding the financial statements of the United States, I must spend a brief moment familiarizing you with the meaning of the three most important words in the financial structure of the United States. No, these three words are not Reagan, prime, and deficit. They are million, billion, and trillion. Everyday we read and hear about millions, billions, and trillions. What are 1,000,000s, 1,000,000,000s, and 1,000,000,000,000s?

From a simple look at the figures, the meaning is obscured by the number of zeros involved. The real meaning is, in fact, hidden from us if we merely think about whether we're talking about six zeros, nine, or twelve.

Here's an example that should enable you to relate better to the magnitude of millions, billions, and trillions. First let's imagine that you were assigned the task of spending $30,000 a day. How long do you think it would take you to spend a million dollars, a billion dollars, and a trillion dollars? At $30,000 a day, it would take approximately 33⅓ days, a little over a month, to spend a million dollars. At that same $30,000-a-day rate, it would take you approximately ninety-one *years* to spend a billion dollars. And in order to spend a trillion dollars, you'd have to spend $30,000 a day for the next *91,300 years*.

So now that we have a handle on millions, billions, and trillions, let's begin to take a look at the financial position of the United States.

First let's look at the assets. They're shown on page 140. As of September 30, 1981, the report reflects total assets of $690.3 billion. As you review the listing of assets, you will see that the first asset is $59.9 billion in cash. This includes $11.2 billion of gold at $42.22 an ounce. At a price of $400.00 an ounce, the value would be increased to approximately $106.1 billion.

Going on to receivables, you find accrued taxes receivable totaling $23.6 billion. Approximately $17.5 billion of this relates to delinquent taxes. Isn't it nice to know that you and I aren't the only ones having collection problems? While the Treasury Department is able to determine the amount of delinquent taxes, it's not able to determine the amount of individual income tax receivable—how much it will actually be able to collect. Since the accrued individual income tax receivable is not reflected as an asset, the effect is to overstate the problem.

The amount of money lost to the Treasury each year because more and more people seem to ignore their tax returns altogether is quite another story. The IRS estimate of tax evasion for the returns *not* filed on April 15, 1983, reached as high as $87 billion. Obviously this is a very large percentage of our recent record deficits, which now seem chronically to be around $200 billion. A graph of the deficit is shown in Appendix A.

Moving down to inventories, one of the omitted notes indicates that, of the total of $113.7 billion, $89.8 billion is inventory of the Defense Department (raw materials, materials and supplies for government use, and stockpiled materials and commodities) and $23.9 billion is for other agencies. The inventory account does not include the value of the weapons stockpile of the United States government because the extent of this inventory item is classified information.

Our land holdings are at cost, but former secretary of the interior James Watt once indicated that a portion of the country's land holdings were worth in excess of $1 trillion. As an aside, the outer continental shelf and other off-shore land as well as the 670 million acres of public-domain lands have not been included in these financial statements. In 1972, a committee of the House of Representatives estimated the value of public-domain land to be $29.9 billion, which, at approximately $43.00 per acre (a tenth of a penny per square foot), seems somewhat low to me.

Of the $130 billion in buildings, structures and facilities, $51.3 billion relates to the Department of Defense. Military hardware is valued at $209.4 billion.

The schedule of assets also reflects additional equipment of $81.2 billion, of which $33.9 billion relates to the Department of Defense. This is in addition to military hardware.

Now, how about the liability side. This is on page 141. As you scan the liability and accumulated position section, two things become clear. First, based on a standard business analysis, the United States government is insolvent. In other words, liabilities exceed assets by $2.8 *trillion* dollars.

We are not a very good candidate for a merger.

Now let's analyze our liabilities for a minute. They total over $3.4 trillion dollars, approximately 74 percent of which is represented by almost $2.5 trillion of pension retirement and disability plan payments payable. Adding this to the net borrowing from the public, "the national debt," of $784.4 billion, we have a total of $3.3 trillion.[1] In other words, 95 cents of every dollar owed by the Federal Government is for either accrued pension or national debt obligations.

Of the total national debt, $326.5 billion is due within one year. This means that either it has to be paid off, or refinanced. We all know that, in fact, every year it is refinanced; hence the continuing need to raise the national debt ceiling. It currently exceeds one and a half trillion dollars. When interest rates go up, so does our national interest expense and, in turn, our national debt. The interest expense for previous and new debt in fiscal 1983 exceeded $153 billion, a figure which is more by itself than all of the government's revenue as recently as 1968.

What we really have here is a vicious circle. Since the government is the largest borrower in our economy, the more it needs, all things being equal, the higher the interest rates, because the rest of us have to compete for the leftovers in the capital marketplace. With higher rates, we increase our national interest expense on our huge debt and continuing $200 billion deficits. In 1984, our interest expense was widely reported as the fastest growing component of our deficits. That means a greater need to borrow, and we start all over again.

Looking at the schedule of the pension benefits payable,

1. On May 25, 1983, the Senate voted to raise the national debt ceiling to 1.389 trillion by 51-41. The House, which apparently feared a roll call vote, had previously approved the change on a voice vote. The bill was signed by President Ronald Reagan.

by far the largest portion is for social security, with civilian personnel in second place, and military personnel in third.

It begins to appear, based upon what we've seen so far, that the United States government has two significant aspects of its business: providing defense and providing retirement benefits.

Let's look again at the accumulated position of the United States government. It's rather interesting to note that not only does the accumulated position at the end of the period reflect 1981's deficit of $76.3 billion, it also includes a "prior period adjustment" to social security of a loss of $188.4 billion. This means basically that the deficits of prior years have been *understated* regarding social security. The adjustment amounts to hearing the bad news after the fact. Experts say that the accounting method for social security requires additional study. Such an adjustment makes it obvious that the present methods aren't telling the story as it is happening.

If private businesses were operated in a manner similar to what these statements suggest is happening, I doubt that the bankruptcy attorneys could handle all of the action. However, some would say it's not fair to analyze the financial statements of the United States government in the same manner as those of a private company. What I can answer is that, while I don't claim to be an economist, it seems to me that something has to give when we operate with deficits in each and every year for almost a generation (twenty years or so), save but one.

Now let's look at our income statements, starting with where the revenue comes from, as may be seen on page 142. For the year ended September 30, 1981, the revenue of the United States government totaled $685.5 billion. Of this amount, $603.2 billion (almost 88 percent of the total) was levied under the government's sovereign power to tax.

Note the difference between the amount of revenues raised through individual income taxes ($285.6 billion) as compared to corporate income taxes ($58.7 billion). More than four times as much taxes are raised from the taxation of

individuals as is raised from the taxation of corporate enti-
ties. Naturally, these figures spark quite a continuing debate.

Of course, this information is subject to different inter-
pretations. Some will look at the figures and say that the
"rich" pay their fair share, and that those who assert otherwise are either ill-informed or willfully distorting the facts.
Others will say that the figures prove only that the giant
corporations have succeeded in keeping their taxes down by
shifting the burden to the broad middle class.

Another hotly debated area is the manner in which our
elected officials spend the tax monies they take in. Where
does all the money go?

In fiscal 1981, federal government expenditures totaled
$761.8 billion. Let's put this into perspective. In one year
there are 31,536,000 seconds. When we correlate the expenditures with this figure, we see that in 1981 the federal government spent $24,157 per second. Let's stop and think
about this for, say, five seconds. One thousand one. One
thousand two. One thousand three. One thousand four. One
thousand five. During this pause, the federal government has
spent, based on 1981 figures, over $120,000. That's quite a
clip—over $2 billion a day.

But what did they spend it on? There are three ways to
look at it. You can look at these expenditures by function, by
object, or by agency.

I think all of this is a little clearer when you look at the
expenses by agency (page 144). When looking at this, you
can see that a large portion of the federal government's expenditures are for national defense and health, education,
and welfare. And we also can see that, contrary to some popular notions, more money is spent on people-related services
than on national defense. In 1981 we spent $168.8 billion on
national defense while we spent $272.5 billion on health,
education, and housing and urban development.

If you wanted to reduce or eliminate our annual deficit,
the first logical places to study would be the areas where the
largest expenditures are made. It is pretty common to hear
the cry to cut defense spending. But since we are spending

even more on health, education, welfare, and housing, it's only logical to look there too.

There are also those who want to take a broad-brush approach to this problem and simply cut the budget by 10 or whatever percent across the board. While politically this is an easy approach to the problem (goring everybody's ox equally), it may not be the wisest. What needs to be done is to cut each budget item after deciding its relative importance and the effect of a cut. This is hard to do because all of the budget categories have their respective constituencies.

In any case something needs to be done. It doesn't seem possible that we can go on operating with constantly increasing deficits. The deficit in 1983 was approximately eleven times larger than it was in 1973, only ten years earlier. And speaking of deficits, we now come to one which makes everything else we've discussed pale by comparison—the deficits of the social security system.

Let's go on to look at social security and the retirement plans for military personnel and federal civilian employees. They are shown on page 145. The first important line is the calculated accrued liability as of September 30, 1981. For social security, that comes to $1,430,000,000,000. Dollars. A trillion and a half for short. The military liability was $377.8 billion and the civilian employee liability was $464.4 billion. That's a total liability of well over $2 trillion. Accrued liability. Well, that's what we owe. How much have we put away to pay that debt? The answer to that lies on the line called total assets of the trust fund. There we find that in the social security fund we have $28 billion and in the civilian fund we have $84.1 billion, or a total of $112.1 billion. That leaves us with an unfunded debt of over $2 *trillion*.

Now let's look at a schedule for projected cash receipts and disbursements on page 150. Here is our one exception. This schedule accompanied the September 30, 1979 statement. When we look at this schedule, and let's concentrate on social security for the time being, we find that for the twenty-five years ending in the year 2003, the anticipated cash receipts will be almost $9.5 trillion and the anticipated disbursements will be almost $7.7 trillion. This would appear to leave us in pretty good shape. We'll be ahead by $1.8 trillion. However, we know that our social security fund was forced to borrow money during 1982, so it is apparent that the 1979 figures were unreliable. The September 30, 1980 financial statements confirm that assumption. If I've failed to knock you off your chair so far, I think one figure on the 1980 statement will, but I'm going to save it for the socko ending.

When we look at the next twenty-five-year period, which runs through the year 2028, we find that the income is $47.8 trillion and the disbursements are $46.2 trillion. So once again we appear to be OK. When we get down to the last twenty-five-year period (from 2029 to 2053), however, we find that income is projected to be $129 trillion and the outgo is going to be $229 trillion. Fifty years from now, we are anticipating a *$100-trillion cash shortfall.*

I promised you a socko ending, and if I haven't numbed you out so far, this disclosure should do it.

Let's focus on the bottom line for social security. The 1979 figures show that total expenditures over the seventy-five-year period will exceed receipts by $97 trillion. Then a year went by. In 1980, the shortfall was projected at $192 trillion (on page 149), an increase of almost 100 percent. The magnitude of that increase—$100 trillion dollars —is beyond anyone's comprehension. That increase is fifty times the gross national product in any single year, at least at today's level of economic activity. We'd have to run $100 billion deficits for *one thousand years* to come up with a disparity as large as $100 trillion.

In 1982, it looked as if the social security system as we knew it had no chance to make it. Of course, the way things turned out, Congress didn't punt. They literally passed the buck from one generation to the next. The social security rescue plan adopted in March 1983, involves tax increases and spending reductions of $165 billion for the 1980s and nearly $2 trillion over the next seventy-five years. Payroll taxes, paid both by employers and employees, will go up from 6.7 to 7 percent in 1984, to 7.05 percent in 1985, and increasingly upward to 7.65 percent in 1990. The wage base on which taxes are levied, which now has a ceiling of $35,700, will go up automatically with the national average increase in wages. The nine million people who are self-employed face increases in rates from 9.35% to 11.3% in 1984, to 11.8% in 1985 and to 12.3% in 1986.

In addition to the taxes, the benefit payments are being deferred and diminished beginning in the year 2000. The age for full retirement will go up from sixty-five to sixty-six by the year 2009. When 2017 rolls around, the retirement age will start rising again. It will be sixty-seven by the year 2027. If any of us want early retirement at age sixty-two, the benefits will be only 70 percent of the full pension, down from the 80 percent presently available.

The third component of the rescue plan is a tax on the benefits themselves. There will be income tax on a single person if half of his or her social security benefit, when added to other income, exceeds $25,000. For a married couple, there will be a tax only if half of their benefits plus other income exceeds $32,000. The somewhat tarnished silver lining is that the tax can only go as high as half of the social security benefits paid.

Actually there will have to be many more changes. It's important to realize that we *have* a two-trillion-dollar problem over the next seventy-five years. The burden is primarily on the "baby boom generation," those of us born between 1946 and 1964. Those at the leading edge of the baby boomers, born in 1946, will be 62 in 2008. During the next twenty-five years or so, the baby boomers will be in their forties, fifties, and sixties. They'll pay higher taxes during their most productive, highest-earning years. When they retire, they will have to live with decreased benefits. While this "solution" may seem unfair, it may be our only way out of this and our deficit problem. I predict that the baby boomers will come to identify with Churchill's battle cry: *"Never have so many been asked to pay so much for so long."*

UNITED STATES GOVERNMENT CONSOLIDATED STATEMENT OF FINANCIAL POSITION AS OF SEPTEMBER 30, 1981 AND 1980 [In billions] [Notes Omitted]

Assets

(What the Government owns—resources that are available to pay liabilities or to provide public services in the future)

	1981	1980
Cash and monetary reserves		
Operating cash in the Treasury	$18.7	$21.0
International monetary reserves	19.7	16.8
Other cash	21.5	16.6
	59.9	54.4
Receivables (net of allowances)		
Accounts receivable	14.4	11.0
Accrued taxes receivable	23.6	26.0
Loans receivable	185.5	159.7
Advances and prepayments	6.1	10.6
	229.6	207.3
Inventories (at cost)		
Goods for sale	24.1	21.0
Work in process	1.4	1.1
Raw materials	3.5	3.6
Materials and supplies for government use	65.6	47.9
Stockpiled materials and commodities	19.1	14.5
	113.7	88.1
Property and equipment (at cost)		
Land	12.5	12.1
Buildings, structures, and facilities	130.0	122.0
Military hardware	209.4	189.5
Equipment	81.2	57.3
Construction in progress	32.4	28.3
Other	3.1	2.5
	468.6	411.7
Accumulated depreciation	(231.3)	(204.0)
	237.3	207.7
Deferred charges and other assets	49.8	32.5
Total	$690.3	$590.0

UNITED STATES GOVERNMENT CONSOLIDATED STATEMENT OF FINANCIAL POSITION AS OF SEPTEMBER 30, 1981 AND 1980 [In billions] [Notes Omitted]

Liabilities

(What the Government owes—liabilities incurred in the past that will require cash or other resources in the future)

	1981	1980
Accounts payable	$97.8	$81.6
Unearned revenue	22.8	17.5
Borrowing from the public	784.4	708.9
Accrued pension, retirement, and disability plans		
Military personnel	377.8	348.9
Civilian employees	464.4	430.3
Social security	1,430.0	1,241.7
Veterans compensation	192.7	174.6
Federal employees compensation	9.9	10.0
	2,474.8	2,205.5
Loss reserves for guarantee and insurance		
programs	7.6	8.7
Other liabilities	59.5	59.7
Total	3,446.9	3,081.9

Accumulated Position

	1981	1980
Accumulated position beginning of period ..	(2,491.9)	(2,169.7)
Current period results	(76.3)	(142.4)
Current noncash provision for social security	(188.4)	(179.8)
Accumulated position end of period	(2,756.6)	(2,491.9)
Total	$690.3	$590.0

UNITED STATES GOVERNMENT CONSOLIDATED STATEMENT OF OPERATIONS FOR THE YEARS ENDED SEPTEMBER 30, 1981 and 1980 [In billions]

Revenues	*1981*	*1980*
Levied under the Government's sovereign power		
Individual income taxes	$285.6	$244.1
Corporate income taxes	58.7	63.9
Social insurance taxes and contributions	186.4	160.7
Excise taxes..............................	40.8	24.3
Estate and gift taxes	6.8	6.4
Customs duties	8.1	7.2
Miscellaneous............................	16.8	15.1
	603.2	521.7
Earned through Government business-type operations		
Sale of goods and services	26.8	19.9
Interest	19.6	13.9
Other	35.9	32.1
	82.3	65.9
Total.................................	685.5	587.6

Expenses by function (see also summary of expenses by object and agency)		
Administration of justice	4.0	3.6
Agriculture	7.2	3.7
Commerce and housing credit	1.2	6.9
Community and regional development	8.6	8.0
Education, training, employment, and social services	25.6	27.5
Energy...................................	11.1	7.8
General government........................	12.9	12.2
General purpose fiscal assistance	13.6	17.7
General science, space, and technology........	4.9	5.2
Health	70.0	61.6
Income security		
Military personnel	42.6	56.1
Civilian employees	52.8	75.9
Social insurance	156.4	127.5
Veterans compensation	31.0	31.8
Other	58.3	52.4

UNITED STATES GOVERNMENT CONSOLIDATED STATEMENT OF OPERATIONS FOR THE YEARS ENDED SEPTEMBER 30, 1981 and 1980 [In billions]
Expenses by function (cont'd.)

Interest	78.4	59.9
International affairs	22.1	19.5
National defense	120.2	110.1
Natural resources and environment	14.4	15.1
Transportation..............................	20.2	19.0
Veterans benefits and services	6.3	8.5
Total...................................	761.8	730.0
Current period results	$(76.3)	$(142.4)

UNITED STATES GOVERNMENT CONSOLIDATED STATEMENT OF OPERATIONS FOR THE YEARS ENDED SEPTEMBER 30, 1981 and 1980 [In billions]

SUMMARY OF EXPENSES BY OBJECT AND AGENCY

Expenses by object	1981	1980
Salaries and employee benefits	$104.8	$96.4
Vendor services and supplies	129.7	111.9
Depreciation	27.3	23.6
Pensions, health and life insurance	128.3	168.8
Casualty insurance and indemnities	171.3	152.7
Grants, subsidies, and contributions	122.0	116.7
Interest	78.4	59.9
Total	761.8	730.0

Expenses by agency	1981	1980
Legislative branch	1.3	1.2
Judicial branch	.7	.6
Executive branch		
Office of the President	17.3	15.2
Departments		
Agriculture	63.1	52.9
Commerce	3.2	4.4
Defense	168.8	177.0
Education	15.7	12.8
Energy	11.6	7.6
Health and Human Services	237.9	197.6
Housing and Urban Development	18.9	15.7
Interior	3.6	4.1
Justice	3.7	4.4
Labor	31.2	31.4
State	2.3	2.5
Transportation	23.5	21.4
Treasury: Interest	78.4	59.9
Other	10.1	13.3
Independent agencies	70.5	108.0
Total	$761.8	$730.0

Schedule VII. ANALYSIS OF PENSION AND RETIREMENT PLANS AS OF SEPTEMBER 30, 1981
[In billions]

Liabilities	Social security	Military personnel	Civilian employees	Other
Accrued liability, September 30, 1980	$1,241.7	$348.9	$430.3	N/A
Add:				
Accruals	333.0	42.6	48.8	N/A
Deduct:				
Benefits paid	144.7	13.7	14.7	N/A
Accrued liability, September 30, 1981	$1,430.0	$377.8	$464.4	N/A
Accrued liability, September 30, 1981	$1,430.0	$377.8	$464.4	N/A
Cumulative trust fund transactions through end of period				
Receipts	1,168.7		208.8	N/A
Outlays (net of unamortized discount and premium on investments)	1,140.7		124.7	N/A
Total assets of the trust fund	28.0	———	84.1	N/A
Liability net of trust fund balance. September 30, 1981	$1,402.0	$377.8	$380.3	N/A

145

Schedule VII. **ANALYSIS OF PENSION AND RETIREMENT PLANS AS OF SEPTEMBER 30, 1981 (cont'd)**
[In billions]

Projected cash receipts and disbursements	Number of years covered	Social Security		Military personnel	Civilian employees		Other
		Percent of taxable payroll	*Amount*	*Amount*	*Contribution rate (percent)*	*Amount*	*Amount*
Cash receipts							
1981	1	10.81	$138.4		7	$28.3	N/A
1982–1985	4	10.94	761.8		7	134.1	N/A
1986–1995	10	12.39	4,367.8		7	526.6	N/A
1996–2005	10	13.85	10,050.5		7	927.8	N/A
Subtotal	25		15,318.5			1,616.8	N/A
2006–2030	25	14.16	76,364.0		7	5,855.1	N/A
2031–2055	25	8.78	187,042.9		7	22,537.0	N/A
Total			278,725.4			30,008.9	N/A
Cash disbursements							
1981	1	11.33	144.7	$ 13.9		18.1	N/A
1982–1985	4	11.17	774.8	71.8		94.6	N/A
1986–1995	10	10.62	3,679.1	288.3		400.3	N/A
1996–2005	10	10.40	7,471.9	506.6		706.5	N/A
Subtotal	25		12,070.5	880.6		1,219.5	N/A
2006–2030	25	13.83	80,585.3			4,576.2	N/A
2031–2055	25	17.00	397,697.1			18,943.3	N/A
Total			490,352.9	880.6		24,739.0	N/A
Net receipts or (disbursements)			$(211,627.5)	$(880.6)		$5,269.9	N/A

Schedule VII. ANALYSIS OF PENSION AND RETIREMENT PLANS AS OF SEPTEMBER 30, 1981 (cont'd.)

[In billions]

Beneficiaries	Plan year									
	1981	1980	1979	1978	1977	1976	1975	1974	1973	1972
Number receiving benefits (thousands)										
Social security	36,006	35,619	35,125	34,587	34,084	33,024	32,085	30,854	29,872	28,345
Military personnel	1,346	1,306	1,263	1,220	1,175	1,129	1,070	1,007	946	890
Civilian employees	1,780	1,675	1,637	1,583	1,508	1,432	1,372	1,306	1,192	1,092
Other plans	N/A	N/A	N/A	N/A	N/A	N/A	N/A	N/A	N/A	N/A
Average monthly benefits (dollars)										
Social security	337	297	258	229	211	194	179	162	143	137
Military personnel	860	766	713	626	583	539	486	424	387	364
Civilian employees	822	784	608	604	527	495	439	366	308	276
Other plans	N/A	N/A	N/A	N/A	N/A	N/A	N/A	N/A	N/A	N/A

N/A Not available.

Schedule VII. **ANALYSIS OF PENSION AND RETIREMENT PLANS AS OF SEPTEMBER 30, 1980**
[In billions]

Liabilities	Social security	Military personnel	Civilian employees	Other
Accrued liability, September 30, 1979	$1,061.9	$303.9	$368.7	N/A
Add:				
Accruals	304.3	56.9	74.9	N/A
Deduct:				
Benefits paid	124.5	11.9	13.3	N/A
Accrued liability, September 30, 1980	$1,241.7	$348.9	$430.3	N/A
Accrued liability, September 30, 1980	$1,241.7	$348.9	$430.3	N/A
Cumulative trust fund transactions through end of period				
Receipts	1,034.1		180.6	N/A
Outlays (net of unamortized discount and premium on investments)	1,001.1		107.0	N/A
Total assets of the trust fund	33.0		73.6	N/A
Liability net of trust fund balance. September 30, 1980	$1,208.7	$348.9	$356.7	N/A

Schedule VII. **ANALYSIS OF PENSION AND RETIREMENT PLANS AS OF SEPTEMBER 30, 1980 (cont'd)**
[In billions]

Projected cash receipts and disbursements	Number of years covered	Social Security		Military personnel	Civilian employees		Other
		Percent of taxable payroll	Amount	Amount	Contribution rate (percent)	Amount	Amount
Cash receipts							
1980	1	10.56	$120.9		7	$20.5	N/A
1981–1984	4	10.82	669.2		7	93.1	N/A
1985–1994	10	12.18	3,949.2		7	345.2	N/A
1995–2004	10	13.85	9,350.3		7	575.1	N/A
Subtotal	25		14,089.6			1,033.9	N/A
2005–2029	25	14.24	72,749.3		7	3,374.6	N/A
2030–2054	25	9.05	182,438.9		7	10,086.3	N/A
Total			269,277.8			14,494.8	N/A
Cash disbursements							
1980	1	10.87	124.5	$ 11.9		13.3	N/A
1981–1984	4	11.24	694.8	62.1		67.1	N/A
1985–1994	10	10.67	3,393.6	256.5		275.8	N/A
1995–2004	10	10.40	6,993.1	440.1		465.6	N/A
Subtotal	25		11,206.0	770.6		821.8	N/A
2005–2029	25	13.57	74,755.8			3,037.6	N/A
2030–2054	25	16.98	375,220.4			9,808.2	N/A
Total			461,182.2	770.6		13,667.6	N/A
Net receipts or (disbursements)	9/30/80		$(191,904.4)	$(770.6)		$827.2	N/A

Schedule VII. **ANALYSIS OF PENSION AND RETIREMENT PLANS AS OF SEPTEMBER 30, 1979**
(Fragment) [In billions]

Projected cash receipts and disbursements	Number of years covered	Social Security		Military personnel	Civilian employees		Other
		Percent of taxable payroll	Amount	Amount	Contribution rate (percent)	Amount	Amount
Cash receipts							
1979	1	10.25	$106.4	$ 10.8	7	$18.9	$N/A
1980–1983	4	10.81	588.5	56.5	7	88.3	N/A
1984–1993	10	12.20	2,825.8	241.3	7	327.2	N/A
1994–2003	10	13.84	5,975.7	416.4	7	547.7	N/A
Subtotal	25		9,496.4	725.0		982.1	N/A
2004–2028	25	14.61	47,801.7		7	3,226.8	N/A
2029–2053	25	9.92	129,145.2		7	9,663.8	N/A
Total			186,443.3	725.0		13,872.7	N/A
Cash disbursements							
1979	1	10.36	107.6	$ 10.8		12.1	N/A
1980–1983	4	10.45	567.7	56.5		51.5	N/A
1984–1993	10	10.59	2,427.8	241.3		259.6	N/A
1994–2003	10	10.67	4,587.2	416.4		443.7	N/A
Subtotal	25		7,690.3	725.0		776.9	N/A
2004–2028	25	13.26	46,208.9	—		2,884.7	N/A
2029–2053	25	16.30	229,742.0	—		9,393.8	N/A
Total			283,641.2	725.0		13,055.4	N/A
Net receipts or (disbursements)			$(97,197.9)	$(725.0)		$817.3	N/A

CHAPTER 23

The National Debt and
How to Eliminate It

In this chapter, I would like to tell the story of how the feudal Japanese approached a national fiscal crisis, one which reminds me somewhat of our own difficulties. I repeat this story almost word for word from an interesting book by Isaiah Ben-Dasan called *The Japanese and the Jews* (John Weatherhill, 1972), with the kind permission of the publisher and the author.

During World War II, at the request of an American organization, Ben-Dasan made a thorough study and translation of a book called *Higurashi Suzuri* by Onda Moku. Ben-Dasan, an orthodox Jew born and raised in Japan, considers it the best available text for the understanding of Japanese political thinking. It is short and concise and completely uninfluenced by European political philosophy. Its author was not a man of letters but simply a skillful manager setting out to write a straightforward book.

Furthermore, since "Higurashi Suzuri" deals with the limited holdings of a small clan, the results of the policies adopted in it are as clear as if they had been produced in a

laboratory test tube. Though Onda's methods and techniques are of a kind that no Jew or European would dream
of employing without modification, they are set forth with
such clarity that anyone can readily understand them:

> Entrusted with the rehabilitation of the Yamashiro clan,
> whose lands were located in what is now Nagano Prefecture,
> Onda (1711–1762) instituted a far-reaching system of re-
> forms including installment plan tax payments and public
> suggestion boxes in which the common people could deposit
> appeals to the clan lord.
>
> In 1756, floods and earthquakes so ravaged the lands of
> the Yamashiro clan that the inhabitants and the lord's family
> were in grave financial extremities. The vast sum they bor-
> rowed from the shogunate did not ease their situation. Ulti-
> mately all of the farmers in the area and, surprisingly, all foot
> soldiers as well, went on strike. (This may well be the first
> page in the history of strike movements in Japan.) At the
> time of Onda's story, the clan was headed by Sanada Yuki-
> toyo, a bright young man who had become lord at the age of
> thirteen. To solve the serious difficulties that faced him in his
> sixteenth year, he singled out Onda, one of his humbler re-
> tainers, to straighten out the clan's financial affairs.
>
> Onda tried to decline the responsibility offered by Yuki-
> toyo, but when he found that he would not be permitted to
> escape the task, he said that he would undertake it if the fol-
> lowing conditions were met. First, he wanted a written clari-
> fication of his duties and rights. Second, no one was to be
> permitted to contradict him, and no one—neither the highest
> of the retainers nor any of the other clan officials—would be
> allowed to disobey his orders. In return for these conditions,
> Onda set for himself a five-year term of office and promised
> to face any punishment prescribed should he fail.
>
> Upon returning home after his interview with the lord,
> Onda announced that he intended to take only light food
> and that he would order no new clothing. He further said
> that he would divorce his wife, disinherit his children, sever
> connections with his relatives, and dismiss all of the people he
> employed. When his surprised associates asked his reasons for
> these drastic measures, Onda said that he intended to speak
> only the truth in the future and that he could not afford to

run the risk of being blamed for the chance slip or lie of a family member or employee. In short, he felt that he would be unable to carry out the needed reforms if so much as the shadow of a doubt about his veracity hung over him. But after having thought about what he said, all of his relatives and associates, vowing to limit their diets and to speak only the truth, pleaded with him to leave things as they were. On the basis of their promises, he relented. In taking this step, Onda obtained the confidence of his followers by assuring them that orders would not be arbitrarily altered and that things would always be done as promised.

Next, Onda called all of the clan officials together and said that, though payments of stipends (i.e., taxes) had been in arrears or sometimes evaded entirely, he intended to see that they were paid accurately in the future. In return he instituted a system of sure rewards and certain penalties. In other words, those who were careless in their public service would meet unfailing punishment. He then ordered village headmen (today, union leaders), rich farmers (the business community), and police officials (the military) to gather and to bring with them those who would speak their minds well and clearly. On the appointed day, all of the officials, beginning with the chief retainers, assembled and sat in rows in the main hall. Onda Moku, after summoning certain representatives of the farmers, said as follows:

"I was called to Edo (the feudal name for Tokyo) into the presence of our lord, with all of his relatives seated before him, and there I was ordered to assume the duties of financial controller of the lord's domain. Although I requested permission to decline, it was not granted, and I have therefore accepted the task. I do not, however, think that my strength alone is sufficient. For that reason I have called you together to discuss this matter. First I ask that you listen to what I have to say; then you may all say what you want.

"I realize that because of the lord's financial predicament many of you have been caused a great deal of trouble. It may well be that in the future, as I attempt to fulfill my role as financial controller, you will be caused still further trouble, and for that I am sorry. But first of all I promise to propose nothing that is impossible; once I have made a statement I will not alter it. I want you to understand this clearly.

Further, unless you and I discuss all matters openly with each other, it will be impossible to put the clan's financial situation in order. Since I cannot succeed by myself, I ask that all of you talk everything over with me freely. This is my first request of you.

"Next, if you are not convinced that what I am doing is right, my work becomes impossible; and I will have no recourse but to commit suicide as custom demands. Whether I am able to do my work smoothly and successfully or whether I must kill myself as a result of failure depends on you. Please let me hear what your feelings are on this point. Of course, I realize that it may be difficult for you to answer now and in this place. Answer me after you have returned to your villages and have talked the matter over with the other farmers."

Then all of the farmers present said that, since in the past the falsehoods of officials and arbitrary alteration of instructions and information had caused them much distress, they were all extremely happy to hear Onda's proposed policy. Onda in turn replied that he was most satisfied that everyone was convinced. He then continued:

"Next, not only on auspicious occasions but also at all other times, I will allow no sending of gifts, no matter how inexpensive. I will not term such gifts bribes, since that would create difficulties for everyone."

On hearing this, all the farmers said that this was a greater blessing than they had expected. Onda went on to say the following:

"In the future I intend to hear everyone's requests and pleas; therefore, there is no need to send bribes to anyone. This goes for all officials as well as for the farmers.

"The next point concerns tax collection. In the past, one hundred from each one thousand available foot soldiers have been kept in the castle for various jobs. Each month the remaining nine hundred were sent to the villages to collect tribute rice. But from now on this practice will cease. Will this cause you distress?"

To this the farmers replied that nothing could make them happier than to be relieved of the burden of the foot-soldier tax collectors who had been in the habit of bringing trouble and violence to the villages during the five or seven days they spent as gatherers of tribute rice. On this point too everyone agreed and found satisfaction. Onda continued:

"Although it is difficult to predict the distant future, I intend to fill this office for five years. During that time, I will levy no demands on you for regional construction or for various duties in the castle. Will it distress you to be relieved of these duties?"

To this all those present answered that the relief from a variety of burdens only increased their happiness.

Onda then said that he wanted all present to remember carefully that they had agreed to and were satisfied with everything he had proposed up to this point. The next matter would require considerable discussion. Onda then said that he knew that among those present were some farmers who had paid advance tribute rice and in some cases even advances on the advances. He asked why they had done so, and the farmers replied that, though it caused them hardship to meet these demands, the officials had ordered it, and they, the farmers, merely did as they were commanded. They had no way out of the predicament. Onda, on the other hand, said that even in the face of the officials' orders, the farmers would have been correct to refuse to pay anything but the tribute due for the current year.

"Taxes paid are over and done with, and certainly there should be no need to pay in advance. You farmers were foolish to give in so readily, and the officials were cruel and even more foolish than you to rely on your easy compliance with their orders.

"This of course is only abstract theory. In fact, it was the poor financial condition of the clan that made it necessary for the officials to demand advances and advances on advances. Cruelty and avarice were not behind the orders. And you farmers, realizing that it was for the clan's sake and not for that of the officials, paid the taxes, though it distressed you to do so."

He praised all the farmers who had paid advances for being honest and straightforward in their devotion to the clan and said that the lord of such a clan of faithful followers was fortunate indeed.

He then called forth all those who had made loans to the clan and asked whether they had done it as the result of a

desire to make profit by charging interest. These men, however, said that far from making interest on their loans, they
had not succeeded in getting back their principal.

Onda said: "Is that the way it was? If you had said, however, that you did not have the money, even if the order to
lend it had come from Edo itself, you could have gone to the
city and refused to lend on the basis of your lack. The government would not have been within its rights to execute you for
your refusal. The local officials, however, went beyond the
bounds of morality to demand money of you because they
knew you had it and would lend if demanded, even though
they had no way to repay it.

"This, again, is only in theory. The facts of the the matter are these: the clan is in such financial straits that it is impossible for us to fulfill our appointed duties in Edo.
Realizing this, though aware that you would not get the
money back, you lent what you had. Thanks to you, we were
able to do our duty in Edo. You did not lend because of the
strict insistence of the collecting officials but because you
knew it would make possible the successful completion of the
necessary duties in Edo. You have not been repaid because
the clan does not have the money. Our lord is grateful to you
for having made his success possible, but in the future, no
more loans will be required."

For this all the farmers expressed their thanks, and
Onda said that he was pleased they were all in accord with
him.

"Now there are some of you who have not paid your
taxes for some time. Why? In general, farmers who sow seed
and fertilize the land and perform all other agricultural duties at the proper time are able to lead good lives with their
families and to pay their tribute rice as is expected of them. Is
it that you who have not paid did not work enough to scrape
together the required tribute? Are you so lazy as this, even
when there are others who have paid their taxes two years in
advance? People of such impudence are detestable to the extent that I could see them cut into small pieces and still not
appease my anger at their behavior. And why did the officials allow these evaders to get away with their tricks? They
should have wrenched the tribute from them by any means
at hand."

Throughout this speech Onda's face flamed with such anger that all the people present bowed their heads.

"But this too is only in theory. For when it was known that the lord's finances were in bad condition and that there were those who had lent and others who had paid advances on their taxes, people who failed to pay what was expected of them were doubtless the victims of extreme poverty. I am certain that these people too wanted to pay their taxes quickly, but because of long sickness or misfortune they were unable to till the soil properly and therefore had no income. In addition, the officials, taking pity on these people, allowed them to fall into payment arrears without punishment. This is an instance of great sympathy on their part, for which we must be grateful. They realized that no amount of coercion could squeeze the tribute from people who did not have the funds with which to pay. The lack of payment must then become the clan's and the lord's loss and the gain of those who did not pay. Be informed, then, that all unpaid taxes to this point are forgiven. But anyone who fails to pay this year's tributes, though he be stark naked with poverty, will face a punishment worse than death."

All present expressed their understanding and agreement. Onda continued:

"Although we should like to return the advances and the advances on advances that some of you have paid, we lack the funds to do so. Furthermore, as you have heard, we intend to forgive all taxes in arrears to this point. Therefore, I request that all of you who have paid advances accept the loss."

All present answered that they understood and that if, as Onda had promised, no advance payments were to be demanded in the future, they agreed to write off as a loss all of the advances they had paid to that date.

"It makes me extremely happy that you see eye to eye with me. But I have one more request. As I said before, I do not want you to answer me now. Instead I want you to return to your villages and tell the other farmers what I have said. All of you must deliberate on the question together before returning an answer. If you fail to agree, I must commit suicide. Remember that the things I request are these: all advances paid to the present must be written off as losses in favor of the clan, and everyone must pay this year's tax rice without fail. There are some things to take into consideration, however, that make the picture brighter than you might think. I am sure that you have given the matter close calculation, and so have I. Do not forget that all bribes that were customarily paid in the past have been forbidden. This alone will save the villages about 100 koku (Note: a koku is about five bushels) of rice a year. In addition, the foot soldiers who formerly made monthly trips to collect taxes will no longer be lodged on you. This means great savings in the housing and food that you provided. Furthermore, you will no longer be forced to supply people and funds for duties and services to officials. All the savings the eliminations of these burdens to the farmers will amount to about seventy percent of this year's tax assessment. In addition, starting now I should like to put tribute taxes for the Yamashiro clan on a monthly installment basis.

"Whether my work leads to success or to my suicide depends on your willingness to accept my proposals. Please return to your villages and discuss the matter earnestly."

The farmers replied that they were ready to answer immediately but that in accordance with Onda's request they would return to their villages to explain this benevolent and superb plan to their fellow farmers. They felt certain that the plan would be happily received and that they would bring back a favorable answer.

"To those who lent money to the clan," Onda went on, "we should like to return what we owe; but we do not have the funds at present. It may be that some of your children or grandchildren will find themselves in financial troubles or in hard times in the future. We should like to pay the money back to them when it becomes needed, but we will be unable to pay interest. All we can return is the principal. Probably none of you will fail without the return of the loans at the present. For this reason I ask you to lend it to the clan and leave it with the clan until your children or grandchildren need it. This too is a request that I make of you all."

To this the farmers who had lent money said that they had lent it with the intention of helping the clan and did not expect any of it back. But they said that they were very happy and grateful to accept this kind and generous offer on behalf of their children and grandchildren. They said they would be indebted to the clan for this kindness, and some of them even wept as they expressed their gratitude.

Once again Onda expressed his happiness that everyone agreed with him. He then said if any of them had been injured or harmed in any way during the past period of bad political administration they might unhesitatingly write down their complaints, which they might present after sealing them well. The farmers, after stating that they understood, went happily on their way home. The officials, who had been seated in silent attention, blanched at the mention of permission to submit written complaints. There were even some present who thought it advisable to get rid of Onda.

The farmers returned to their villages, called together their neighbors and explained Onda's proposal point by point. The farmers were delighted. They said that the relief they would have from the irksome tax-collecting forages of the foot soldiers was so great a blessing that, in combination with the savings resulting from the removal of duties in connection with the officials and the castle, it would enable them to pay with ease far more taxes than were demanded. Then they insisted that they deliver an answer of agreement as quickly as possible because they wanted to put both Onda's and the lord's minds at rest.

Then the village headmen and the work foremen, in their greetings to the groups, said: "We must hurry to the public office and make known everyone's agreement to Onda's proposal. It will look better for us if we go quickly." Everyone was overjoyed at this, and they then decided to compose the complaints about former abuses that Onda had instructed them to write. Everyone was in the best of moods, for the time had come for them to make clear all the things they had suffered and hated in the past. It was as if a bright moon had suddenly appeared to illuminate the darkest night. There was happiness in each man's heart, for he felt that in the future everything would certainly go well.

After the complaints had been written and the farmers had discussed things among themselves, the village headmen and the leaders of the farmers departed for the public office, where they made the following report:

"When we told the farmers of the proposals, they were overjoyed and grateful. We have resolved to offer to pay two years' advance taxes and to lend other money whenever you may order it as a result of your needs. Please understand our willingness to do these things."

But Onda replied: "Thanks to you, the farmers have agreed. This means that I will be able to fulfill my task without committing suicide. It is thanks to all the farmers. Moreover, when the lord hears that you have willingly offered to pay two years' tribute rice in advance, it will certainly bring him great satisfaction. But it will be sufficient for you to pay only this year's taxes. Your feelings are too profound. I shall tell our lord that you will pay this year's taxes, but there is no need to make an advance.

"On the other hand, you must all work as hard as you can. I am sure that I need not say this, but to do less than your best at your farming tasks is a sin against heaven. Work with diligence at your farming, and do what you like with the time that is left over. In your leisure, indulge in ballad singing, playing the samisen, or gambling; but remember that gambling for money is illegal and that anyone caught at it is liable to the death penalty. As long as no money transactions are involved, it is all right to gamble. In general, unless people have some suitable recreation for their leisure hours, their work will be less effective than it ought to be. For that reason I order you to enjoy yourselves but to work with all your might, too.

"Finally, remember that people who do not believe in the Buddhas and the gods are bound to suffer great hardships. Therefore it is good to believe and to pray for both this world and the world to come.

"Now, did you bring the complaints I told you to write?" asked Onda; and the farmers' representatives replied that they had. Onda then said that they were not for his eyes and that he would present them to the lord. With this he told the farmers to return to their homes and to work with all their might.

He then hastened to the lord, to whom he said: "Please rejoice, for the financial situation is certain to improve. The farmers have agreed to cancel our debts to them. This means that we owe nothing. And starting this month they will pay a full ten thousand koku in rice as taxes. Because they have agreed to pay everything to the very last grain, our financial recovery is certain. No one holds anything against the clan. On the contrary, they are so happy that they volunteered to pay two years' taxes instead of one. I am convinced that it is because of your great kindness and moral virtues that the farmers have consented to go along with my policies and to pay their taxes promptly and accurately."

The lord answered: "No, it is because of your efforts. You have been a faithful retainer worthy of the highest reward." After thanking the lord for his praises, Onda said: "It is now time to examine the petitions containing the farmers' complaints. Please examine them for yourself." And with this he handed them over to the lord.

Later, the lord summoned Onda and said to him: "Look at the complaints that the farmers living in my domain have written. This is what they wrote." And Onda replied after examining the materials: "I knew that this was the kind of thing they would say." The lord then asked what he should do, and Onda answered: "There is no cause for worry. The farmers will adhere to one side or to the other. It depends on the way they are used. They will be good if a good person uses them, but they will be bad if a bad person uses them. Since you are a man of the highest morality and kindness, we have nothing to worry about. It is true that the officials against whom the farmers have complained deserve death for their wickedness, but since they are men of talent who are needful to us now, I suggest you call them before you and with a kind aspect instruct them in this way: tell them that though you have entrusted the financial recovery of the clan to me it is impossible for me to attend to all details. Therefore, they must help me in my tasks. Tell them too that they must follow my instructions and, doing their work in agreement with my wishes, discuss all things with me."

The lord then asked if such a step would not interfere with the successful accomplishment of Onda's own work. Onda denied that it would hinder him in any way. After saying that he would do as Onda wished, the lord called in his officials and with a mild face instructed them as Onda had said. To these instructions they all agreed gratefully and readily. The clan's fiscal crisis was avoided and a fairer, stabler and more efficient means of financing the government was begun.

The problem of *our* national debt is far beyond the scope of this book. What I'm suggesting, however, is that the solution lies not so much in the mechanics as in the way we go about considering and adopting a solution.

It's hard to imagine what it would be like to have a balanced budget instead of annual deficits of $200 billion. But if the federal government were substantially out of the marketplace for borrowed funds, interest rates might fall. The prime would be so low that we wouldn't have to worry about borrowing below it. Until then, however, the more you know about borrowing money, the less it will cost you.

Charts

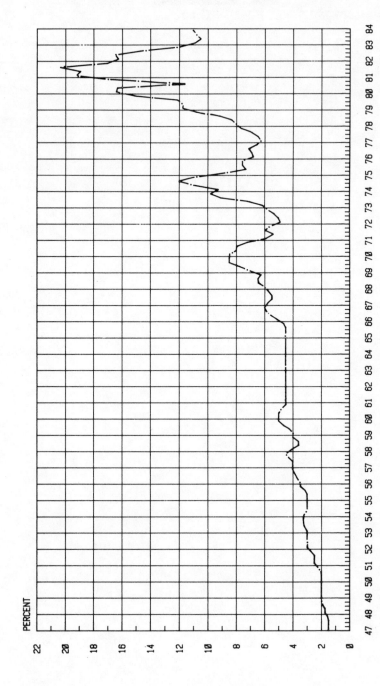

PERCENT

PRIME RATE

164

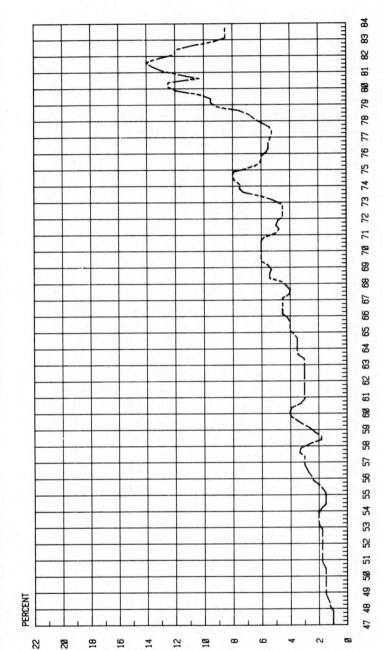

Discount rate

165

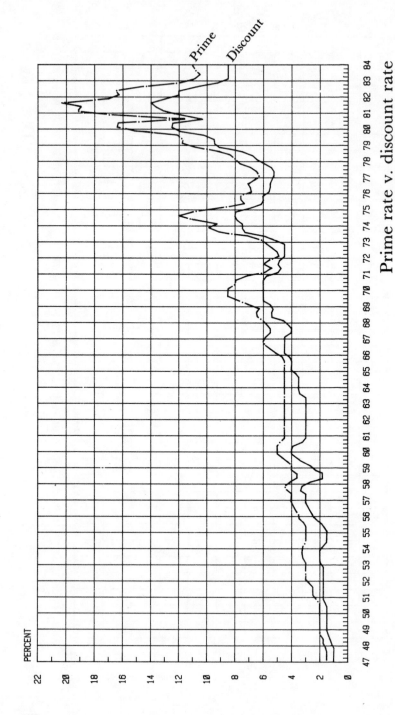

Prime rate v. discount rate

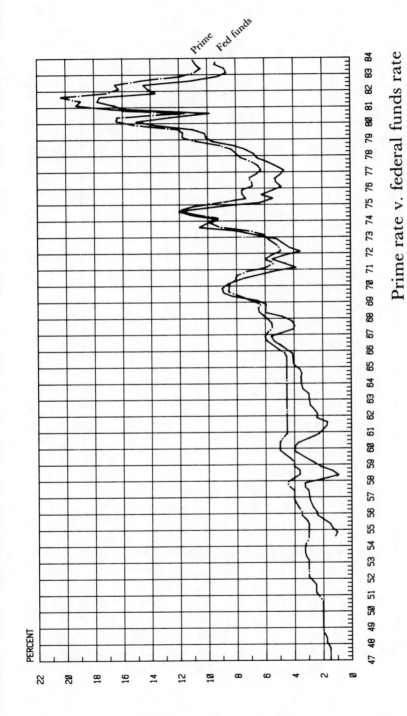

Prime rate v. federal funds rate

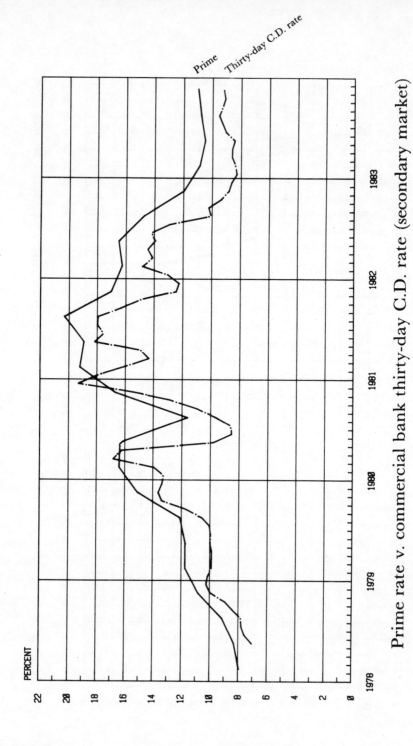

Prime rate v. commercial bank thirty-day C.D. rate (secondary market)

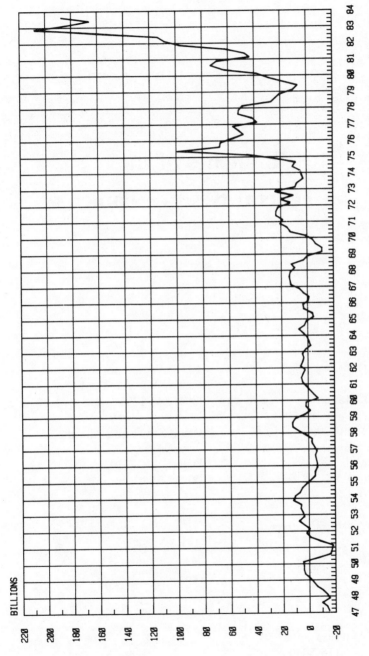

BILLINGS

UNITED STATES FEDERAL DEFICIT

Branches of the
Federal Reserve Bank

Northeast

P.O. Station
New York, NY 10045
(212) 791-5000

600 Atlantic Avenue
Boston, MA 02106
(617) 973-3000

100 North 6th Street
Philadelphia, PA 19105
(215) 574-6000

South

104 Marietta Street NW
Atlanta, GA 30303
(404) 586-8500

4th and Franklin Street
Richmond, VA 23261
(804) 643-1250

Wood Street and Allard
  Street
Dallas, TX 75201
(214) 651-6111

West

P.O. Box 7702
San Francisco, CA 94120
(415) 544-2000

Midwest

P.O. Box 834
Chicago, IL 60690
(312) 322-5322

East 6th and Superior
   Avenue
Cleveland, OH 44114
(216) 241-2800

250 Marquette Avenue
Minneapolis, MN 55480
(612) 340-2345

Federal Reserve Station
Kansas City, MO 64198
(816) 881-2000

P.O. Box 442
St. Louis, MO 63166
(314) 444-8444

Glossary

Acceleration clause: A clause allowing the lender to accelerate the due date, so that the full balance owing becomes due immediately. The clause can be invoked if the borrower encumbers the property, sells it, goes into default, or files bankruptcy, depending on the wording.

Account analysis: The practice in some banks of computing the cost of maintaining a checking account, usually based on collected balances versus account activity. Excess cost may be passed on to the customer as a service charge.

Annual percentage rate: An interest rate that is calculated in such a way as to make all contracts comparable by interest rate no matter what the term, dollar amount, or type of loan.

Automatic overdraft account: A checking account that, when overdrawn, automatically creates a loan that pays the overdraft, subject to a prearranged credit agreement between the bank and the depositor.

Average daily balance: The average daily balance in a deposit account, which can be computed in many ways but usually by adding together the closing balance each day for a month and dividing by the number of business days in the month. Also called the average ledger balance.

Balance sheet: A statement listing assets and liabilities to arrive at the net worth (positive or negative) of a person or a business.

Bank: The odd economic definition is "any institution that lends money," but modern usage has refined this to any institution, chartered by an arm of state or national government, that handles deposits and withdrawals and grants loans. A non-bank bank is an institution carrying out either one of these functions, but not both.

Base rate: The term used by Citibank which is analogous to the prime rate quoted by others.

Beneficiary: A person who is named to receive the proceeds of an insurance policy, trust, or estate.

Borrower: Any individual or business that receives funds or services in consideration for future repayment.

Cash value: The cash amount that could be received if an insurance policy or asset was sold or the policy surrendered.

Collected balance: The amount actually received from another financial institution and cleared into a customer's account.

Compensating balances: A phrase with no definition. Checking and savings accounts are compensating to a bank.

Credit card: A method of obtaining money, goods, and services on credit using a plastic card of a lender and drawing on an established line of credit.

Credit life insurance: Insurance offered by lending institutions that insure the liquidation of the unpaid balance on a loan upon the death of the borrower.

Credit rating: A person's or business's credit history, along with present and future financial status, used as a measure of ability and willingness to repay obligations.

Credit union: A financial institution, federally or state chartered, that performs consumer banking functions for members of a specified group as defined by its charter.

Default: The act of failing to meet the payments of a financial obligation.

Deficiency: A term used when an asset pledged as collateral is repossessed and sold to repay a loan, but there still remains a balance to be repaid.

Demand deposit: A deposit payable on demand to the depositor or to his or her order. Funds in checking accounts are demand deposits.

Demand loan: A loan with no set maturity date, but which is payable in full upon demand by the lender.

Depositor: A customer of a bank who deposits funds.

Discount rate: The rate, expressed as a percentage, that is charged by the Federal Reserve Banks for loans made to member banks.

Equity: The difference between the fair market value of a property and all claims or liens against it.

Federal Deposit Insurance Corporation (FDIC): The regulatory agency that supervises state banks that are not members of the Federal Reserve. The FDIC also insures depositors' accounts at most banks for up to $100,000.

Federal Reserve Banks: Quasi-governmental agencies that regulate credit and the money supply through dealings with commercial banks.

Federal Reserve Notes: The United States' current paper money currency, based on the assets of the Federal Reserve Banks.

Federal Reserve System: The central banking system in the United States that issues money and performs services on behalf of banks and the federal government.

Federal Savings and Loan Insurance Corporation (FSLIC): The federal agency that insures depositors' funds at those savings and loan associations that are included under the organization's coverage.

Float: That part of the customer's deposits for which the funds are uncollected. Thus, while the total balance includes the float, that is not the amount the depositor's bank has actually received from other banks.

Finance charge: The amount charged by a lender for the extension of credit.

Foreclosure: A procedure used to sell property upon the default of the borrower.

Garnishment: A court order requiring an employer to pay part of a debtor's wages to the court for the benefit of a creditor.

Interest: The amount paid for the use of money over time. Banks pay interest to savings depositors for the use of the funds on deposit, and borrowers pay interest to banks for the use of the money advanced to them.

Lien: A claim on property to secure the payment of a debt.

Line of Credit: An agreement by a bank to extend credit to a customer up to a predetermined limit. The bank can modify the agreement or withdraw from it if the borrower has a change in financial status.

Liquid asset: An asset that can be quickly converted into cash.

Loan: The extension of credit with an agreement or contract promising future repayment. Usually the borrower signs a promissory note, agreeing to pay back the funds at a certain date and with a certain amount of interest.

Maker: The person who signs a check or note; the person who promises to pay an obligation when due.

Maturity: The date when a note or other obligation becomes due and payable.

Mortgage: A loan secured by real property.

Mutual savings bank: A bank that is owned by its depositors and accepts savings deposits. There are about 500 mutuals in the United States, most of which are located in New England and New York. In modern operation, they offer personal checking accounts or NOW accounts, as well as savings accounts; and many make personal loans, though the bulk of their lending is in first home mortgages.

National bank: A commercial bank with a federal charter; identified by the phrase "National Association" (N.A.) or "National Trust and Savings Association" (N.T. & S.A.).

National Credit Union Administration (NCUA): The federal agency that supervises federal credit unions and insures depositors' funds in federal and certain state-chartered credit unions.

Negotiable instrument: An unconditional written order or promise to pay money, which can be transferred from one person to another. A check is the most common form of negotiable instrument.

Net worth: The excess of assets over liabilities. An individual's net worth is the total value of what he owns minus the total amount of what he owes.

Night depository: A service offered to business customers whereby they can place money in a secure place until banking hours when it can be counted and deposited. This creates a "bailee-bailor" relationship.

Nonmember bank: A bank that does not belong to the Federal Reserve System. All national banks must belong to the Federal Reserve System. Membership is optional for state banks.

Pledged assets: Assets frozen because they are being used as security for a loan.

Point: One percent of an amount borrowed that is charged as a fee for making the loan.

Prepayment penalty: A charge by the lender when a borrower chooses to repay a mortgage before its actual due date.

Prime rate (old definition): The lowest rate, expressed as a percentage, that is charged by commercial banks for loans made to those larger business borrowers that have the highest credit ratings. Hence, it is supposed to be the best rate offered. The prime rate is *not* set by the Federal Reserve Bank. *(New definition):* The rate announced from time to time by a bank as its prime rate.

Promissory note: Also referred to as a note. A written promise made by one person to pay a certain sum of money on demand or at a future specific or determinable date to another person.

Reference rate: The rate charged by the Bank of America which is analogous to the prime rate quoted by other banks and to the base rate quoted by Citibank.

Repossession: The act of reclaiming the pledged collateral of a defaulted loan.

Right of offset: The right of a bank to use any demand balances deposited at the bank to cover a defaulted obligation of the owner of the account.

Savings account: A time-deposit account, with or without a passbook. Two common types, regular and special-notice or ninety-day investment accounts, make up the bulk of this service.

Savings and loan association: A financial institution that performs most consumer banking functions, but that specializes in all types of savings accounts and home mortgage loans.

Secured loan: A loan secured with collateral.

Service charge: A fee for service (processing checks, deposits, stopped checks, etc.). In banking, this is usually the charge applied against a customer's account for maintaining a checking account. See "Account analysis."

Single-payment loan: A loan where the entire balance is due in one payment; the maturity is usually at thirty, sixty, or ninety days. Accrued interest is paid on maturity.

Spread: The difference between two interest rates.

State bank: A commercial or mutual savings bank with a state charter.

Statement: A written summary of all banking transactions in an account during a certain period of time, usually one month, that is prepared by a bank for the customer. Originally this term referred to a customer's statement of his checking account, but recent computer advances have made it feasible to provide statements for savings accounts as well and, in many cases, for all banking transactions, including loans and credit cards.

Statement of condition: A detailed listing of a bank's assets, liabilities, capital, and net worth as of a specific date. The major statement issued by a bank is the year-end statement, although quarterly reports are also available.

Time deposit: A deposit for which notice to withdraw funds technically may be required. Savings accounts are time deposits, though notice is seldom required on regular accounts. Certificates of deposit and special-notice accounts, however, either specify a maturity date or require notice for withdrawal.

Traveler's checks: Special checks sold to travelers with an insurance feature that protects the buyer against loss if the checks are lost, stolen, or destroyed.

Uncollected funds: That part of the customer's balance for which checks deposited have not cleared for payment. See "Float."

Unit bank: A single independent bank that has no branches but conducts all of its business at one office.

Unsecured loan: A loan where no collateral is pledged and which is made on the signature and based on the credit rating of the borrower.

Usury rate: A rate of interest that is above the maximum legal rate. The usury limitations vary from state to state.

Bibliography

Ben-Dasan, Isaiah. *The Japanese and the Jews.* New York: John Weatherhill, Inc., second paperback printing, 1982.

Cohen, Herb. *You Can Negotiate Anything.* New York: Bantam Books, 1982.

Cook, Timothy Q., and Bruce J. Summers (ed.). *Instruments of the Money Market.* Federal Reserve Bank of Richmond (5th edition, 1981).

Jones, Landon Y. *Great Expectations: America and the Baby Boom Generation.* New York: Ballantine, 1981.

Mayer, Martin. *The Bankers.* New York: Ballantine, 7th edition, 1983.

Norton, Joseph Jude, and Sherry Castle Whitley. *Banking Law Manual.* New York: Matthew Bender, 1983.

Ouchi, William G. *Theory Z.* New York: Avon Books, 1981.

Ringer, Robert J. *Looking Out for #1.* New York: Fawcett Crest, 1977.

Ritter, Lawrence S., and William L. Silber. *Money.* New York: Basic Books, Inc. 1970.

Stigum, Marcia L., and Rene O. Branch, Jr. *Managing Bank Assets and Liabilities.* Dow Jones-Irwin, 1983.

Index

About the Author

Nelson E. Brestoff graduated from U.C.L.A. in 1971 with a Bachelor of Science degree in engineering. He was one of twenty honors seniors and one of three Rhodes Scholar nominees. He received his Master of Science degree in environmental engineering science from the California Institute of Technology in 1972 and spent a summer as an intern with the National Materials Policy Commission in Washington, D.C. In 1975, he graduated from the University of Southern California Law Center where he was a member of the Law Review. After law school, Mr. Brestoff was a Deputy City Attorney for the City of Los Angeles for two years and since then has been in private practice.

Mr. Brestoff's law office is in West Los Angeles, where he emphasizes real estate and business transactions and litigation. He is also the owner of Southwest Escrow Corporation in Inglewood, California.

Besides the U.S.C. Law Review, his writing has appeared in the *Los Angeles Times* and the *Town Hall Reporter,* a magazine published by Town Hall of California. He has served on the California Attorney General's Environmental Task Force, the board of directors of the Planning and Conservation League from 1973 to 1977, and from 1979 to 1983 on the board of directors of the West Los Angeles Regional Chamber of Commerce.